Y0-BCU-304

Developing Language
and Literacy

Developing Language and Literacy

Effective Intervention in the Early Years

Julia M. Carroll, Claudine Bowyer-Crane,
Fiona J. Duff, Charles Hulme,
and Margaret J. Snowling

Illustrations by Dean Chesher

WILEY-BLACKWELL

A John Wiley & Sons, Ltd., Publication

EAST NORTHPORT PUBLIC LIBRARY
EAST NORTHPORT, NEW YORK

This edition first published 2011
© 2011 John Wiley & Sons Ltd.

Wiley-Blackwell is an imprint of John Wiley & Sons, formed by the merger of Wiley's global Scientific, Technical, and Medical business with Blackwell Publishing.

Registered Office
John Wiley & Sons Ltd, The Atrium, Southern Gate, Chichester, West Sussex, PO19 8SQ, UK

Editorial Offices
The Atrium, Southern Gate, Chichester, West Sussex, PO19 8SQ, UK
9600 Garsington Road, Oxford, OX4 2DQ, UK
350 Main Street, Malden, MA 02148-5020, USA

For details of our global editorial offices, for customer services, and for information about how to apply for permission to reuse the copyright material in this book please see our website at www.wiley.com/wiley-blackwell.

The right of Julia M. Carroll, Claudine Bowyer-Crane, Fiona J. Duff, Charles Hulme, and Margaret J. Snowling to be identified as the author of this work has been asserted in accordance with the UK Copyright, Designs and Patents Act 1988.

All rights reserved. No part of this publication may be reproduced, stored in a retrieval system, or transmitted, in any form or by any means, electronic, mechanical, photocopying, recording or otherwise, except as permitted by the UK Copyright, Designs and Patents Act 1988, without the prior permission of the publisher.

Wiley also publishes its books in a variety of electronic formats. Some content that appears in print may not be available in electronic books.

Designations used by companies to distinguish their products are often claimed as trademarks. All brand names and product names used in this book are trade names, service marks, trademarks or registered trademarks of their respective owners. The publisher is not associated with any product or vendor mentioned in this book. This publication is designed to provide accurate and authoritative information in regard to the subject matter covered. It is sold on the understanding that the publisher is not engaged in rendering professional services. If professional advice or other expert assistance is required, the services of a competent professional should be sought.

Library of Congress Cataloging-in-Publication Data

Developing language and literacy : effective intervention in the early years / Julia M. Carroll ... [et al.].
    p. cm.
  Includes bibliographical references and index.
  ISBN 978-0-470-71186-6 (cloth) – ISBN 978-0-470-71185-9 (pbk.)
  1. Language arts (Preschool)–United States. 2. Reading (Preschool)–United States. 3. Children–Books and reading–United States. I. Carroll, Julia M.
  LB1140.5.L3D48 2011
  372.6–dc22

                 2010036220

A catalogue record for this book is available from the British Library.
Set in 10.25/12.5pt Arial Font by Thomson Digital, Noida, India
Printed in Singapore by Ho Printing Singapore Pte Ltd

1   2011

Contents

List of Figures

List of Tables

List of Boxes

List of Boxes

About the Authors

All authors made an equal contribution to the book.

Claudine Bowyer-Crane is a Senior Lecturer at Sheffield Hallam University and a chartered psychologist. She has a research background in the area of reading and language development and has worked on a number of programmes investigating effective means of intervention for children with reading and language difficulties. She was project manager for the Nuffield Language 4 Reading project and was responsible for the development of the Oral Language Intervention Programme.

Julia M. Carroll is an Associate Professor at the University of Warwick, where she has been since 2004. She completed her PhD in Developmental Psychology at York in 2001. Her interests lie in reading and language development, and particularly in how phonological skills link to language and to literacy. She was responsible for the development of the Phonology with Reading Intervention.

Fiona J. Duff is currently a Post-Doctoral Research Fellow in the Department of Psychology at the University of York, specialising in theoretically-motivated reading and language interventions. As recipient of the British Psychological Society Postgraduate Award, she was seconded to the Parliamentary Office of Science and Technology in 2009 where she prepared a briefing note for parliamentarians on theoretical and policy issues related to teaching children to read.

Charles Hulme is Professor of Psychology at the University of York. He has conducted research on a wide range of developmental disorders. He was the joint recipient of the Dina Fietelson Award of the International Reading Association for research on reading intervention in 1998 and is past editor in chief of *Scientific Studies of Reading*. His current research focuses particularly on interventions to ameliorate children's reading and language difficulties.

Margaret J. Snowling is Professor of Psychology at the University of York and a chartered clinical psychologist. She served as a member of Sir Jim Rose's Expert Advisory Group on Provision for Dyslexia (2009) and is Past President of the Society for the Scientific Study of Reading. Her books include *Dyslexia* (2000), *Developmental Disorders of Language, Learning & Cognition* (2009) and *Dyslexia, Speech & Language* (2006).

Foreword

In recent years we have seen unprecedented progress in understanding how children learn to read and of the factors that give rise to children's reading difficulties. These gains owe much to research stemming from cognitive developmental psychology and neuroscience.

This book represents the work and expertise of an internationally recognised team of researchers whose work consistently focuses on meeting the most important professional needs: securing teachers' knowledge and successful pedagogical practice in the teaching of reading to typically developing children as well as those with stubborn developmental difficulties in learning to read.

The book skilfully distils the findings of robust research and clearly sets out the implications of those findings for professional practice. It is a major contribution to the work of teachers and teaching assistants, and those who train them.

Jim Rose

Acknowledgements

The research we report in this book was funded by the Nuffield Foundation. Many people offered us help and support with the project. First and foremost we would like to thank all the schools and teaching assistants who took part and without whom this work would not have been possible. Our teaching assistants were: Maggie Aitken, Kath Batters, Elaine Brown, Shirley Clarke, Jo Edwards, Yvonne Gilbert, Dianne Graham, Phillipa Gregory, Jemma Guilliat, Rita Hooton, Lynn Johnson, Anne Lockitt, Maureen Maltby, Kerrie Martin, Paula Meads, Andrea Muir, Gemma Murray, Carol Rushby, Trina Turner, and Jo Whitehead from the following schools in York and North Yorkshire: Barwic Parade Primary School, Braeburn Infant and Nursery School, Carr Infant's School, Cayton Community Primary School, Clifton Green Primary School, Friarage Community Primary School, Gladstone Road Infant School, Hinderwell Community Primary School, Huntington Primary School, Mill Hill Community Primary School, New Earswick Primary School, Overdale Community Primary School, Poppleton Road Primary School, Robert Wilkinson Primary School, Selby Abbey Primary School, Selby Community Primary School, St Peter's RC Primary School, Westfield Community Primary School, Yearsley Grove Primary School. The smooth running of the project was greatly facilitated by our colleagues in York and North Yorkshire LAs particularly Glynnis Smith and Simon Gibbs and through the involvement of speech and language therapists especially Gill Clarke and Louise Bodkin.

The research that we conducted drew on the expertise of colleagues and students. We acknowledge our collaboration with Jeremy Miles who advised on all things statistical. We are indebted to Elizabeth Fieldsend who was with us from the outset and in particular, for her support with tutorials. We also thank Louise Nasir and Kristina Goetz for their valuable input to the design of the interventions, Janet Hatcher for tutorial support and Pam Baylis, Poppy Nash for running focus groups. Assessments were conducted by Lizzie Bowen, Michelle Cargan, Sarah Edwards, Natalie Falkinder, Ros Francis, Debbie Gooch, Rachel Harlow, Lisa Henderson, Dimitra Ioannau, Kim Manderson, Rachael McCool, Naomi Meredith, Elisa Romeo, Emma Truelove, Jodie Unau, Nicky Vowles, and Meesha Warmington; we are grateful to them.

Finally we would like to thank Christopher Jolly, Jolly Learning Ltd and Alan Henson, Black Sheep Press who generously donated materials, Dean Chesher for his work on the illustrations and Susannah Witts and Lindsey Bowes for administrative support.

The Nuffield Foundation is an endowed charitable trust that aims to improve social well-being in the widest sense. It funds research and innovation in education and social policy and also works to build capacity in education, science and social science research. The Nuffield Foundation has funded this project, but the views expressed are those of the authors and not necessarily those of the Foundation. More information is available at www.nuffieldfoundation.org

Chapter 1

Theoretical Framework: Foundations of Learning to Read

Children vary in the age at which they first start to talk and in the skill with which they use language to communicate. For this reason, it is not unusual for late-talking, speech difficulties or slow language development to go unnoticed in a family, particularly in a first-born child. However, delays and difficulties in speech and language provide some of the first clues that a child is at risk of reading difficulties. This book is concerned with how children with such difficulties can be helped, not only to learn to read, but also to improve their spoken language skills. In this chapter we begin by outlining the structure of spoken language before going on to describe how language skills are the foundation of literacy development and specifically, how the development of reading draws on these skills. We close by considering some of the main characteristics of children who, despite having received good instruction, fall behind their peers in reading development.

THE STRUCTURE OF LANGUAGE

Language is a complex system that requires the coordinated action of four subsystems: **Phonology**, **Semantics**, **Grammar** and **Pragmatics**. *Phonology* is the system that maps speech sounds onto meanings and is critical for reading development, while meanings are part of the *semantic* system. *Grammar* is concerned with **syntax** and **morphology** (the way words and word parts are combined to convey different meanings) and *pragmatics* is concerned with language use.

Developing Language and Literacy: Effective Intervention in the Early Years
By Julia M. Carroll, Claudine Bowyer-Crane, Fiona J. Duff, Charles Hulme, and Margaret J. Snowling
© 2011 John Wiley & Sons, Ltd

An assumption of our educational system is that by the time children start school, the majority are competent users of their native language (but see below).

- They can listen to what people say to them and understand.
- They can follow instructions.
- They can speak clearly.
- They can use language to express their needs.
- They can convey a message to someone else.
- They can take turns in conversation.

These are all reasonable expectations. But for far too many children, poor language at school entry can begin a downward spiral of poor literacy, under-achievement and in the longer term, poor job prospects. Before we consider language skills specifically in relation to literacy development, let us spend some time describing the different language skills children bring to the task of learning. These are vocabulary, **grammar**, **pragmatics** and **phonology**.

Vocabulary

Vocabulary knowledge refers to all of the word forms and meanings that we know and is a key component of language comprehension. Vocabulary is also one of the strongest predictors of educational success. During the pre-school years, typically developing children extend their vocabulary at a very rapid rate, possibly adding around 50 to 70 words to their vocabulary-base each week mostly through conversation. By the time children go to school, they typically have an oral vocabulary of some 14,000 words. However, as Isobel Beck and her colleagues (Beck, McKeown and Kucan, 2002) have pointed out, beyond school age, most conversations contain words that everyone understands and therefore they no longer provide an effective means of promoting vocabulary knowledge. Rather, at this stage, children begin to learn words through reading and explicit teaching.

When a child hears a familiar word, he or she automatically activates its meaning in what is known as a 'semantic representation'. If the child has good vocabulary, they also activate the meanings of related words. Therefore children with good vocabulary are at an advantage in learning: not only do they know the meanings of the individual words they hear but also these words provide them with a context within which to interpret larger units of discourse.

Some words cause particular problems for comprehension in young children or those with language delay. These include:

- question words (*what, who, whom, when, where, how, whose, which, how many, how much, why* (Ripley, Barrett and Fleming, 2001));
- words with more than one meaning (ambiguous words, such as *bat, minute*); and
- homophones (words that sound alike, such as *bear* and *bare*).

Grammatical Skills

Grammar is a system of rules that specifies how words are used in sentences to convey meaning. In order to comprehend, children must be able to use grammatical clues in sentences. Children also use **grammar** to learn the meanings of new words. In a classic example reported by Lila Gleitman (1995) children were shown a picture of someone sifting through a bowl of confetti. How children interpreted the meaning of a nonsense word depended on the grammatical construction of the question they were asked. For example, if asked, 'Can you see any *sebbing*?' (verb), children pointed to the person's hands (where the action was performed). If asked, 'Can you see a *seb*?' (common noun), they pointed to the bowl. If asked, 'Can you see any *seb*?' (mass noun), they pointed to the confetti.

Formally, grammar is made up of **morphology** as well as **syntax. Morphology** refers to the basic structure of words and the units of meaning (or morphemes) from which they are formed; the word '*boy*' is a single morpheme but the compound word '*cowboy*' contains two morphemes, '*cow*' and '*boy*'. In English, there are relatively few compound words of the '*cowboy*' type; however, words like '*camping*' (*camp + –ing*) or '*camped*' (*camp + –ed*) also contain two morphemes and '*decamped*' contains three. Inflections are parts of words that cannot stand alone (e.g., *–ed, –ing, –un*) but when combined with a stem they serve a grammatical function. Verb inflections are particularly important to comprehension – they denote contrasts between for example, past and present tense (walk/walked), singular and plural forms (house/houses). The verb 'walk' is a single morpheme; when it is used to refer to the past, the inflection –ed is added making 'walked' a two-morpheme word. Similarly, to use the verb 'walk' to refer to a man, it is necessary to add the third person singular inflection –s; hence 'he walks'. 'Walks' is also a two-morpheme word (even though it has only one syllable). Figure 1.1 illustrates a task often used to assess children's ability to produce grammatically correct forms of verbs. In the first picture, the girl is picking flowers. The child is asked to say what the girl has done in the second picture: 'She has picked the flowers.'

Figure 1.1 Figure illustrating a task to assess children's ability to produce grammatically correct forms

Pre-school children often have difficulty with grammatical markers like inflections. In particular, they may miss off inflections when referring to third person singular: 'mummy cook'. They may also make mistakes on irregular past tense forms: 'the man *goed* there'.

Syntax refers to the grammatical structure of sentences; different grammatical forms generally take particular semantic roles in the sentence. Nouns usually refer to *agents* or *objects* whereas verbs refer to *actions* or *feelings*. In a similar vein, *prepositions* signify location while *adjectives* and *adverbs* are used to describe nouns and verbs respectively.

Most children have a grasp of simple sentence structure but more complex structures may cause difficulty through the primary school years. More complex constructions include:

- passives, e.g., '*The window was broken by the boy.*'
- embedded clauses, e.g., '*The girl with the red hair ran away.*'
- relative clauses '*The boy who delivered the news was scared.*'

Children also sometimes have difficulties with pronouns. They may often misuse them or have difficulty knowing who or what they refer to, both within a sentence ('*he is in the car*') and across sentences ('*The boy loved his puppy. He put it in the car*').

Pragmatic Abilities

Pragmatics is the system of language which is concerned with communication and specifically, how language is used in context. Efficient communication depends upon the speaker and listener sharing certain assumptions, for example, that communication between them should be both informative and relevant to the topic under discussion. Ideally it should also be truthful, clear, unambiguous and economical. More generally, communication frequently involves looking beyond the precise information stated or beyond its literal interpretation. When people have pragmatic difficulties, their language behavior violates these assumptions: they may talk at length about topics not directly relevant to the present situation or use an inappropriate 'register', such as speaking in an overly formal manner for the context. Perhaps most commonly they get the 'wrong end of the stick'.

Pragmatic failure commonly occurs when the speaker does not take into account the listener's perspective and either provides too much or too little information for them to be able to communicate well. Young children often make social 'gaffes' because of limitations in their pragmatic skills. Generally such pragmatic failure is acceptable in a young child but in older children the failure to take account of the perspective of another person can seem rude or ill-judged. Figure 1.2 shows a child who is having difficulty understanding the use of figurative language when his mother tells him, 'Pull your socks up.'

Phonological Skills

Phonology is the system of language that is concerned with how speech changes denote changes in meaning. For example, there is a very small difference in sound

Figure 1.2   Illustration of pragmatic difficulty

between the words 'bat' and 'pat' but this change signals the difference between something we use to hit a ball and the way we pet a dog. The phonological difference between 'bat' and 'pat' is at the level of the **phoneme**. From a very early age children are sensitive to phonetic cues and they can use these to differentiate word meanings, but they are not aware of **phonemes**. Later when children start to speak, they mark phonemic distinctions but for some time their speech production is immature and so they may be difficult to understand.

For most children, phonological development follows a typical course and some types of speech error are common. Often before their speech becomes fully intelligible at around school age, children omit syllables from words (e.g., they say 'jamas' for 'pyjamas or 'nana' for 'banana'), misarticulate words (saying, for example, mouse for mouth) and miss out consonants from clusters (e.g., 'kate' for 'skate'). Importantly, during the pre-school years, children are not explicitly aware of the internal structure of speech; although they use speech to communicate they do not typically reflect upon it and have only limited ability to manipulate its components.

We usually use the term **phonology** in a rather different way to that discussed above when we consider phonological development in relation to reading. In this context, 'phonological abilities' usually refers to skills that involve reflecting on,

Syllable	CRISP				
Onset - rime	CR	ISP			
Onset - vowel - coda	CR	I	SP		
Phoneme	C	R	I	S	P

Figure 1.3 Segmentation of a syllable into onset-rime and phoneme units

processing and manipulating speech sounds (usually called **phonological aware-ness** tasks). Before reading instruction, children have considerable difficulty with **phonological awareness** tasks that involve **phonemes**. However, a persistent difficulty in segmenting the sounds of spoken words can be an important marker of a specific reading difficulty.

It is generally believed that the development of **phonological awareness** proceeds from large to small units. English has a complex syllable structure. Figure 1.3 shows how a syllable in English can be split into units of different sizes. Thus, all syllables contain a vowel; simple consonant-vowel-consonant (CVC) syllables (e.g., hat) comprise an **onset** (the consonant before the vowel –h-) and a **rime** (the technical term used to describe the unit comprising the vowel and the final consonant or coda - at). In turn, **rime** units can be segmented into phoneme units, namely the vowel (a) and the coda (t). In more complex syllables, both the **onset** and the coda may include consonant clusters (crisp).

The difficulty of a **phonological awareness** task depends on the size of the phonological unit and the nature of the manipulation that is required. Generally tasks involving the manipulation of larger units (e.g., syllables or **rime** units) are easier than tasks involving smaller units (**phonemes**) (Figure 1.4).

Tasks involving the deletion or transposition of sounds within words are typically harder than tasks requiring judgments about the similarity between sounds in words. When thinking about reading instruction, it is important to bear in mind that there is strong evidence that reading development depends upon having well developed **phoneme** awareness; activities involving syllables and rhymes help children to tune into the sounds of words but it is **phoneme** awareness that is critical for learning to read and spell.

LANGUAGE SKILLS AND LEARNING TO READ

It is useful to distinguish *speech skills* from *language abilities* when considering literacy development. Learning to read in an alphabetic system, such as English, requires the development of mappings (or connections) between speech sounds and letters – the so-called *alphabetic principle*. In turn, the alphabetic principle depends on phonemic skills. Wider language skills (vocabulary, **grammar** and

Figure 1.4 Examples from phonological awareness tasks at the level of the syllable, rime, and initial phoneme. In each item, the child sees a cue picture and is asked which of two pictures sounds a bit the same. Panel A shows a syllable level task; jigsaw and seesaw share a final syllable and puppy is the unrelated distractor. In panel B, a rhyme task is shown; mat and bat rhyme and pig is the distractor. In panel C, moon shares an initial sound, while net is a similar-sounding distractor.

pragmatics) are required to understand the meanings of words and sentences, to integrate these in texts and to make **inferences** that go beyond the printed words.

In the early stages of learning to read within an alphabetic system such as English, children's attention is devoted to establishing decoding skills (**phonics**). Later children begin to rely increasingly on word meanings to gain fluency in their reading, and they use broader language skills including vocabulary, **grammar** and **pragmatics** to appreciate both the gist and the detail of what they read. Children with poor oral language remain at risk of poor reading comprehension even though they may be able to accomplish the initial task of word-level decoding. Such children include those whose mastery of English is poor because it is not their mother tongue.

A large number of studies have now followed the progress of children during the early stages of reading development. On the basis of findings from these studies we know a great deal about what predicts individual differences in reading attainment. In one such study conducted by our group (Muter et al., 2004) we followed the early reading development of 90 children between the ages of 4 years 9 months and 6 years 9 months. We assessed each of the children once a year on tests of letter knowledge, word recognition and **phonological awareness**. The tests of **phonological awareness** tapped the ability to detect rhyming relationships between words and also to identify and segment **phonemes**, the smallest units of spoken words. At 4 years of age the children were also given a test of vocabulary and a year later at 5, they completed two tests of **grammar**; one of these required the children to order words to make a sentence and one required them to add morphemes to words (e.g. to make the number 'five' into an adjective – fifth). Finally, we assessed reading comprehension at the end of the study.

The findings of our study are displayed in Figure 1.5 in what is known as a 'path model'. They were clear and quite simple: there were two predictors of individual differences in reading at age 5 – these were **phoneme** awareness and letter knowledge at age 4; and from age 5 to age 6 there were three predictors – **phoneme** awareness, letter knowledge and 5-year-old reading skills. In short, the children who had come to school knowing letters and being able to segment spoken words into speech sounds fared better in learning to read (and the same situation held for learning to spell). As Brian Byrne of the University of New

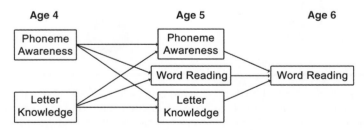

Figure 1.5 Path diagram showing the relationships between pre-school phonological awareness and later word reading skills (after Muter et al., 2004)

England, Australia has argued, these two skills are fundamental to the alphabetic principle (Byrne, 1998).

What then is the role of wider language skills beyond **phonology** in learning to read? To answer this question we can use the findings from our study to discover what predicts reading comprehension (rather than word-level reading skills). When we do this, we find that vocabulary knowledge and grammatical awareness are important predictors of individual differences in reading comprehension, once differences in word-level reading (decoding) are taken into account.

In summary, **phoneme** awareness and letter knowledge are the foundations of word-level reading skills. In turn, word level reading and wider language skills are the foundations of reading comprehension. We can conclude that a range of language skills are vital to literacy development, notably, phonological skills, (specifically **phoneme** awareness), vocabulary knowledge and grammatical ability. It therefore falls to us as educators to ensure that children have well developed spoken language in the early school years to provide a secure foundation for learning to read.

Precursors of Phoneme Awareness in Pre-School

Since this book is concerned with children who have difficulty in acquiring the alphabetic principle, it is important to look further back in development to consider the precursors of **phoneme** awareness skills. In one of the few studies to address this question, we followed the development of **phonological awareness** in 67 children between the ages of 3 years 10 months and 4 years 9 months (Carroll et al., 2003). At three points in time, in addition to a test of letter knowledge, the children completed tasks tapping syllable matching, rime matching and alliteration (first sound) matching (as shown in Figure 1.4). In each task, the child was shown the picture of a target item and then they had to select one of two pictures to match the target in terms of the phonological unit tested. Given the theory that **phonological awareness** proceeds from large to small units, we predicted that syllable matching would be easier than **rime** matching. In fact, the children in this study performed at a similar level when required to match rhymes as syllables but, as expected, they found alliteration matching (which is at the level of the **phoneme**) much more difficult.

We next investigated which early skills could tell us how well children would do on **phoneme** awareness tasks at school entry. We did this by examining the relationships between vocabulary knowledge, awareness of large sound units in words (syllable and **rime** skills), letter knowledge, and how well children could articulate words. At the end of the study we also assessed **phoneme** awareness. We found that awareness of syllables and **rimes** was related to how large a vocabulary the child had and these measures together with the clarity of their speech (**articulation**) together predicted phonemic awareness (as measured by alliteration matching, **phoneme** deletion and **phoneme** segmentation).

We can conclude from this study that children with better developed vocabulary in pre-school had better developed awareness of the phonological units of speech.

It is also noteworthy that children with better developed (more intelligible) speech also tended to fare better on the **phoneme** tasks.

With these findings as a back-drop, we can consider the risk of reading impairments in children who come to school with poorly developed speech and language skills. From our discussion so far it seems likely that difficulties affecting the phonological system of language will affect the development of **phoneme** awareness. Moreover, since learning letter sounds is a phonological learning task, we can expect this also to be affected in children with phonological difficulties. It follows that children with poor **phonology** will be at risk of poor word-level decoding skills, including **phonics**. Speech production difficulties are an additional risk factor for poor reading particularly if these are not resolved by school entry. On the other hand, wider language difficulties place children at risk of reading comprehension difficulties.

The 'Simple View' of Reading

The idea that proficient reading depends on oral language skill is captured in the **'Simple View'** **of reading**, shown schematically in Figure 1.6. According to the **Simple View** (Gough and Tunmer, 1986), reading comprehension is the product of word decoding and linguistic comprehension skills. Decoding is vital to reading comprehension; if a child cannot decode, then he or she will be unable to extract meaning from the written word. However, once words are decoded a child must fall back on his or her oral language comprehension to understand what a writer conveys. It is well recognised that children vary in the ease with which they can

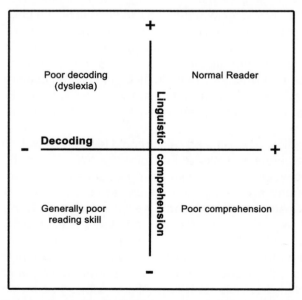

Figure 1.6   The Simple View of Reading (after Gough & Tunmer, 1986).

decode. They also vary in their linguistic comprehension, and consequently in their reading comprehension. A proficient reader has good decoding and good listening comprehension skills, as shown in the upper right quadrant of the figure. Poor reading comprehension can occur with or without poor decoding, as shown in both lower quadrants of the figure.

Decoding Deficits in Dyslexia

Children with **dyslexia** typically have word recognition deficits in the absence of poor comprehension. It is well-established that these children have phonological deficits and a recent independent review of **dyslexia** provision conducted by Sir Jim Rose for the government in England (Rose, 2009) proposed that the main signs of **dyslexia** include poor **phonological awareness**, slow verbal processing speed and verbal short-term memory limitations. By way of illustration, Figure 1.7 (Panel A) shows the performance of children with **dyslexia** on a **phoneme** deletion task in which they had to remove a **phoneme** from a spoken word. Figure 1.7 (Panel B) shows performance in a phonological memory task involving repeating nonwords. In each case, their performance was compared with that of children of the same age (CA-controls) and younger children reading at the same level (RA-controls). The children with **dyslexia** showed impairments on both tasks in relation to the comparison groups confirming they have phonological difficulties.

Surprisingly less well discussed are the phonological learning difficulties of children with **dyslexia**. Kristina Goetz (née Herden) in our group taught children with **dyslexia** a set of Greek letter-names (Herden, 2003). Each letter was shown twice paired with its name, followed by six learning trials with feedback. Figure 1.8 shows the performance of the children with **dyslexia** on the last trial of the experiment and after a short delay. Compared with children of the same age, the

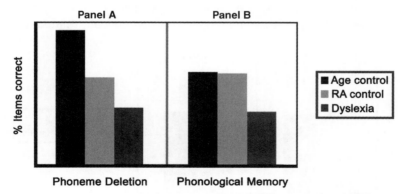

Figure 1.7 Performance of children with dyslexia compared with CA- and RA-controls on tests of phoneme deletion and nonword repetition, showing that the children with dyslexia are impaired (data from Marshall, C. M., Snowling, M. J., & Bailey, P. J. (2001). Rapid auditory processing and phonological ability in normal readers and readers with dyslexia. *Journal of Speech Language & Hearing Research, 44*, 925–940).

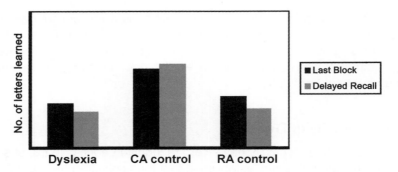

Figure 1.8   Performance of children with dyslexia on the last block of trials of a letter learning experiment and after a short delay; the children with dyslexia learned fewer letters than age-matched (CA) controls (after Goetz, 2003)

children with **dyslexia** learned fewer letters and performed only as well as younger controls. Given the problems children with **dyslexia** have in the two basic components of alphabetic skill (letters and **phonemes**), it is not surprising that they have difficulties developing decoding skills.

Poor Comprehenders

In contrast to **dyslexia**, some children show a reading impairment that specifically affects text comprehension while decoding is unaffected – these children are often referred to as '**poor comprehenders**'. In a series of experiments conducted in our lab (Nation, 2005) we have shown that, while **poor comprehenders** perform normally on phonological tasks, they have problems in the semantic domain of language. Figure 1.9 and 1.10 show data depicting their performance on parallel tasks tapping **phonology** and **semantics**. In Figure 1.9 are the findings of oral fluency in tasks in which they are given a target word (e.g. *man*) and have to generate either rhyming words (*pan, ran, van*) or semantically related words (*boy,*

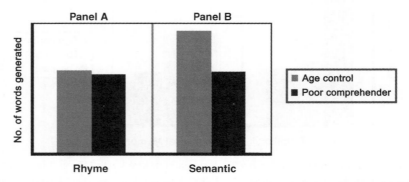

Figure 1.9   Performance of poor comprehenders on a test of oral fluency. The poor comprehenders showed normal rhyme fluency (Panel A) but impaired semantic fluency (Panel B).

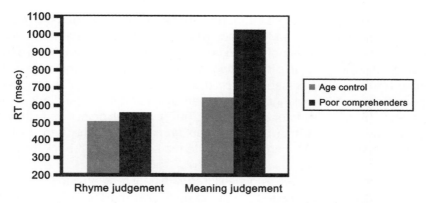

Figure 1.10 Performance of poor comprehenders on tests of rhyme and meaning judgement. The poor comprehenders showed normal rhyme but impaired semantic judgement (data reported in Nation, K., & Snowling, M. J. (1998). Semantic processing and the development of word recognition skills: evidence from children with reading comprehension difficulties. *Journal of Memory & Language, 39*, 85–101).

girl, lady, woman), in a 30-second interval. Although they did fine when generating rhyming words, they produced fewer semantically related associates than typically developing children. In a similar vein, Figure 1.10 shows the findings from a task requiring them to judge whether pairs of spoken words rhymed (e.g. *boat – coat*) or were similar in meaning (e.g. *boat – ship*). Again they performed within the normal range on the rhyme tasks but were impaired in terms of speed and accuracy on the meaning judgement task.

Findings like these have led to the view that **poor comprehenders** have difficulties with language skills beyond **phonology**. We have seen that **poor comprehenders** have poor semantic knowledge, plausibly linked to limitations in their vocabulary knowledge; they also have difficulty with figurative language and the impact of these difficulties is readily observed in their limited use of context during reading. Importantly however, as colleagues Kate Cain and Jane Oakhill (2006) have shown, **poor comprehenders** also have poor knowledge of story structure and conventions and they fail to monitor their own comprehension (for example, they may fail to look back to resolve ambiguities or to correct their reading). Further, a key area of difficulty for **poor comprehenders** is in making **inferences** and integrating information at the level of the text to form a coherent understanding of what they read.

Children at Risk of Reading Difficulties

Although studies of children with **dyslexia** and **poor comprehenders** show that relatively specific difficulties with reading are possible, it is more usual for children to have difficulties with several components of language (and hence literacy). A family study of **dyslexia** conducted by our group (Snowling, Gallagher and Frith, 2003) emphasizes this point. In this study, we followed the progress of pre-school children, recruited just before their fourth birthday up until the teenage years but here we will focus on their early literacy development. The children in the study were considered to be 'at risk' of **dyslexia** because they had a parent with a history of reading difficulties (and it is interesting to note that some 38% of these children were late talkers). We assessed the children at the ages of 4, 6 and 8 years on a large battery of tests of language and reading-related tasks (and later in early adolescence (Snowling, Muter and Carroll, 2007)). At each point in time they were compared with children in a control group from families who had no history of reading impairment but were similar in terms of their social background and economic circumstances.

At 8 years of age, there were more children with poor reading and spelling in the group at family risk of **dyslexia** than in the comparison group. We defined poor literacy here as having literacy skills significantly below the average of the control group. In relation to this norm, 66% of the family sample were affected (only about 10% of the control group showed such difficulties). We then proceeded to look retrospectively at the patterns of early language that characterized the different groups, namely, the at-risk poor readers (who we will refer to as dyslexic), the 'at risk' children who became normal readers, and the control group (removing four cases of **dyslexia**). At 4 years, the oral language development of the dyslexic children was slow compared with that of the two normal reader groups, and at 6 years, they were already showing difficulty with phonological awareness tasks. Figure 1.11 shows performance of the three groups on tests of early literacy skill at age 4 and 6 years. Here the picture is different. As expected, the children with **dyslexia** were impaired in letter knowledge and on a test of phonic skill (literally the number of words they were able to write correctly in a spelling test). However, the performance of the 'at risk' children who went on to be normal readers was also less good than that of controls; it was midway between that of the controls and the children with **dyslexia** on the test of letter knowledge and as poor as the dyslexic group on the phonetic spelling test.

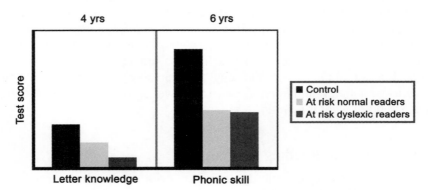

Figure 1.11   Performance of children from 'at risk' and control groups on tests of early literacy. The 'at-risk' children who went on to be normal readers at 8 showed early literacy problems; their letter knowledge was moderately impaired at 4 years and they were impaired in translating between graphemes and phonemes at 6 years (Snowling et al., 2003).

In summary, children from 'at risk' families who went on to be classified as 'dyslexic' had difficulties during the early years on a wide range of language measures including **phonological awareness**, vocabulary and expressive **grammar**; they were also slow to learn their letters, arguably the first sign of '**dyslexia**'. The 'at risk' children who went on to be normal readers were almost as poor as the children with **dyslexia** in tasks tapping phonological skills and they were moderately impaired in letter knowledge, but their (non-phonological) oral language development was normal. We think that the reasons these children did not succumb to reading difficulties at 8 years was because they were able to use their good language skills to get around the phonic decoding deficit they experienced, and hence to 'compensate'.

It follows that the risk of reading impairment is not all or none. Among the children we studied whose parents were dyslexic, there were a number of different outcomes which ranged from a global reading impairment affecting both word-level decoding and reading comprehension to normal fluent reading. It seems that the developmental outcome for a child at risk of poor reading depends not only on how severe their phonological difficulties are, but also on the other language skills they bring to the task of learning. Those who have good vocabulary and wider language skills are likely to be able to compensate better, modifying the risk they carry of becoming dyslexic.

Children with English as a Second or Additional Language

One particularly disadvantaged group in the English education system is children learning English as an additional language. In England, Government statistics published in 2009 (DCSF, 2009a) indicate that 15.2% of pupils in UK primary schools and 11.1% of pupils in UK secondary schools were learning English as an additional language (EAL). For many of these children there is a persistent attainment gap relative to peers who have English as a first language (DCSF, 2009b). Researchers investigating the literacy development of children learning EAL consistently report a profile similar to that of **poor comprehenders** – in other words, they tend to have difficulties with both listening and reading comprehension in spite of adequate decoding skills. As such their difficulties can go largely unnoticed in the classroom. The work of researchers including Jane Hutchinson from the University of Central Lancashire, Helen Whiteley from Edge Hill University and Kelly Burgoyne from Down syndrome Education International suggest that the difficulties experienced by children learning EAL largely stem from weak vocabulary skills. In a longitudinal study following children with EAL from Year 2 to Year 4, Jane Hutchinson and colleagues (Hutchinson et al. 2003) consistently found lower levels of reading and listening comprehension, **expressive** and receptive vocabulary, and grammatical skills for children with EAL compared to their monolingual peers. Importantly, **expressive** vocabulary in Year 2 significantly predicted performance in reading and listening comprehension in Year 4 for children with EAL but not their monolingual peers.

CONCLUSIONS

We began by considering the structure of language and distinguished the role of speech and of language skills in the development of reading. We argued that speech skills (**phonology**) are the foundation of word recognition processes in reading while broader language skills are critical to reading comprehension. At the core of reading difficulties are phonological problems, though children with good language skills beyond **phonology** may be able to use these to 'bootstrap' their ineffective phonic skills. In contrast, children with poor language are at high risk of reading comprehension impairments (Bishop and Snowling, 2004).

The intervention programme described in this book aims to foster skills at the foundations of literacy in the hope of enabling children who enter school 'at risk' of reading difficulties to close the gap between themselves and their peers. It builds on research conducted over a number of years by our group, initially pioneered by Peter Hatcher (Hatcher, Hulme and Ellis, 1994) in a county-wide study in Cumbria, and subsequently developed for implementation in mainstream classrooms, as a catch-up programme and for small group teaching for children with reading difficulties. We review the findings of these background studies in the next chapter, before turning to the current research.

Chapter 2

The Importance of Evidence

In writing this book we had several aims in mind. One aim was to convey how an understanding of the nature and causes of children's language and reading difficulties leads directly to recommendations for teaching. If our understanding of the nature and causes of children's difficulties is correct, then methods of teaching designed to overcome the causes of these difficulties should 'work'. This in turn provides evidence to suggest that our ideas about the causes of children's problems are correct. In contrast, sometimes our ideas may not be correct and hence the related methods of teaching will not work well; this therefore should lead us to question our ideas about what is causing the problem in the first place. We refer to this idea as a 'virtuous circle' (Figure 2.1) between theory and practice: good theories lead to ideas for teaching; if teaching works this supports and strengthens the theory; if teaching does not work as we expect, this should lead us to question our ideas, and possibly revise our theory about what the problem is.

HOW CAN WE EVALUATE THE EFFECTIVENESS OF TEACHING METHODS?

The approach of taking theory through to practice requires us to evaluate the effectiveness of different approaches to teaching: how do we assess whether a method of teaching works? The most obvious (and regrettably most widely used) method is with a before/after or pre-test/post-test study. In this method, we simply measure a group of children's reading skills before an intervention is given and then re-test all the children (say 6 months later) after they have received a period of specialist teaching. Suppose in this case children start with severely deficient

Developing Language and Literacy: Effective Intervention in the Early Years
By Julia M. Carroll, Claudine Bowyer-Crane, Fiona J. Duff, Charles Hulme, and Margaret J. Snowling
© 2011 John Wiley & Sons, Ltd

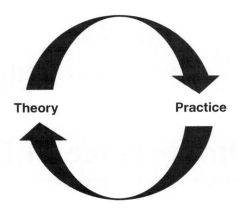

Figure 2.1   The virtuous circle

reading skills, and after the intervention we find they are close to being average readers for their age. It is tempting to conclude from this that the intervention has 'worked' and produced the large increases in reading skill that are observed. Unfortunately, we cannot conclude anything from this sort of study. There are two reasons for this which are usually referred to by the technical terms 'temporal change' and 'regression to the mean'.

The first issue is the most important and easiest to explain. The point is simply that children's reading skills may change for many different reasons (their usual teaching, help from parents, changes in motivation). So studying a single group, all of whom get the same help, can never show that the help received has worked – it may be that these children would have shown improved reading skills if we had done nothing. This is a very basic point that we must not forget when evaluating interventions.

The second issue, 'regression to the mean', is more difficult to understand; this refers to the fact that if we select people for having extreme scores on some measure, when those same people are reassessed on the same measure, they will tend to obtain scores that are nearer the average level. So, people with very poor scores will tend to get better scores when re-tested; conversely people with very good scores will tend to get worse scores – both sets of people end up with less extreme scores on re-test. Such effects will be greater for measures that are less accurate or reliable; but unless a measure is totally reliable (and no measures in education or psychology are) we can always expect re-test scores to show regression to the mean.

The basic message is that we cannot evaluate an intervention without a 'control' group who receive no intervention (or possibly an alternative intervention). There may be different ways of forming control groups, but it is now generally accepted that the best way to do this is to use random assignment of people to the treatment and control groups. This method has been used for a long time in science, but it is sometimes seen as arising from studies in agriculture, and has been extensively used and refined in medicine. The method is sometimes referred to generically as 'Experimental' but more usually is called '**Randomised Controlled Trial**' (or **RCT** for short), when we are evaluating the effect of a treatment.

RANDOMISED CONTROLLED TRIALS

In a randomised study people are assigned 'at random' to either receive an intervention or to be in a control group. The simplest design is where the control group receive no treatment; but sometimes they receive the treatment later (when the treatment of the first group is complete). More complicated designs may involve the control group receiving an alternative treatment; this is potentially a conservative assessment of the effects of an intervention, unless the alternative intervention really is totally unrelated to the issue we are studying. An excellent overview of the details of **RCT** methods and how to conduct them is given in David and Carole Torgerson's book *Designing Randomised Trials in Health Education and the Social Sciences* (Torgerson and Torgerson, 2008).

The importance of random allocation was noted and thoroughly developed by the great statistician Ronald Fisher, in the context of agricultural experiments. Fisher was concerned with understanding, for example, the effects of fertilizer on the growth of plants. If we believe a fertilizer works, we would need to apply it to several different plots of land and observe how well a particular plant grows in the plots with and without the fertilizer. How do we decide which plots to apply the fertilizer to? Suppose we had a large area of land, and we could create 100 plots. One way would be to take the 50 plots on one side of the area and put fertilizer on them. It is immediately obvious, however, that this is not a good way of doing things – perhaps one side of the area is closer to a river that provides a source of ground water, or is affected by other influences, that can affect how well plants grow. The point is that the 100 plots may differ in innumerable ways that will affect plant growth, and furthermore, some of the differences between the plots we may not know about (e.g., levels of an unknown trace element in the soil). Fisher's great insight was that if we pair plots with treatments at random, we do not need to know how the plots differ, because using random assignment will ensure that (on average) all pre-existing differences will even out.

Following closely on from Fisher's work in agriculture, Austin Bradford Hill was arguably one of the most influential figures in promoting the use of random assignment of treatments to patients in medical trials. Here exactly the same logic applies as in the case of agricultural trials. We believe that a certain drug is effective in preventing death from a disease, but patients who suffer from this disease may differ in numerous ways, some that we can easily measure (e.g., age, weight, gender, social class) and others that we may not know about (e.g., genetic constitution). Again if we use random assignment, on a sufficiently large sample of people, any pre-existing differences between people in the treatment and no-treatment groups should even out – giving us a fair (unbiased) estimate of the likely effect of the drug on the disease. In drug trials it is common to give people in the control group a 'placebo' or inactive pill, which controls for the possibility that expectations of getting better from the drug may account for part of the effect observed.

Once this idea of random assignment is understood we can see that it applies (and should be used) in numerous areas including education, health, social policy and criminal justice. If we want to know if an intervention works, using random assignment of people to the intervention or non-intervention group gives us the most certain basis for establishing how effective a treatment is. For this reason, **RCTs** have come to be seen as the 'gold standard' for evidence in medicine, because they give the most certain basis for establishing that an intervention causes a change in an outcome.

ALTERNATIVES TO RCTS

RCTs are simple and elegant ways of demonstrating that a particular intervention works; and if an intervention is going to be widely used in health or education it is reasonable for us to demand that policy should be based on this type of evidence. Sadly, it remains the case that often educational interventions are promoted without this sort of evidence. In some rare cases it may be difficult or impossible to conduct an **RCT**. In such cases there are alternative procedures (often referred to as quasi-experimental designs) that can give us reasonable, but not water-tight, evidence that an intervention works.

Historical comparisons involve comparing data from different groups before and after a particular intervention or policy is implemented. For example, if the method of teaching reading changed in a particular local education authority, we might measure the reading skills of children in the local authority in two consecutive years (before the new method of teaching was introduced, and the year after it was introduced). If reading standards are better in the second cohort of children this *suggests* that the new method of teaching is better – but of course other things might have changed to account for the improvement. So we can never be sure of the correct interpretation for historical comparisons.

Case-control studies involve comparing a group who have received an intervention with a matched group who have not received the intervention. For example we might compare the reading scores of children given a reading intervention, with other children matched for reading levels who were never offered the intervention (perhaps from other schools who did not have access to the intervention). Positive effects of an intervention in a case control study again suggest that the intervention is effective – but once again there are numerous other reasons for the apparent effects. For example, reading might just be generally less well taught in the schools that were not offering the intervention, or the non-intervention children might be disadvantaged in other ways, any of which might lead to an apparent, but not 'real', effect of the intervention.

One other design is the so-called interrupted time series design. At the present time, we are not aware of this design being used in studies of reading. However what it would consist of is measuring reading (or language) repeatedly before introducing a change such as a new method of teaching reading (or training language); we would then measure the same thing repeatedly after the change. If we find stable scores before the change that are lower than stable scores after the change this again suggests that the change has affected reading (or language). But again we need to try to exclude other possible reasons for the change occurring.

In summary, randomised (sometimes called experimental) studies give the best evidence for the effectiveness of an intervention.

EVIDENCE FROM RANDOMISED TRIALS FOR THE EFFECTIVENESS OF DIFFERENT INTERVENTIONS FOR READING PROBLEMS IN CHILDREN

Reading Intervention

As we described in Chapter 1, there is evidence that learning to read aloud depends critically upon two skills that are developing around the age when children start school: **phoneme** awareness and letter-sound knowledge. **Phoneme** awareness is the ability to identify the individual sounds in a spoken word. Letter-sound knowledge refers to a child's ability to supply the correct sound for letters of the alphabet. Together these two skills enable a child to understand the alphabetic principle: the fact that in alphabetic languages like English, letters in printed words typically map onto individual sounds in spoken words. These ideas lead us to expect that children who are having difficulties learning to read are likely to have problems with these basic foundations, and the evidence is that they do. Given this background we should expect that interventions which address these two foundations should help children who are struggling to learn to read. The evidence broadly supports this idea.

During the past 20 years, there have been two important influences on the teaching of reading and spelling to children with difficulties. The first is *Reading Recovery* associated with Marie Clay in New Zealand (Clay, 1985), and the second is **phonological awareness** training. These two approaches are very different. In its original incarnation Reading Recovery de-emphasised phonology and phonic skills. Instead Reading Recovery stressed the importance of reading practice guided by an experienced teacher, who noted a child's difficulties, and provided structured feedback to correct these difficulties. The second approach, concerned with **phonological awareness**, aimed to prevent the development of reading difficulties in young children by ensuring they had well-developed phonological skills. In contrast to Reading Recovery this approach, in its pure form, involved no reading at all, but instead focused on developing the child's phonological skills as a foundation for learning to read. There was evidence that both of these approaches were effective to some degree, though it was notable that the effects of phonological training alone were small. In Bradley and Bryant's classic study (Bradley and Bryant, 1983), the effects of phonological training alone (which was based on **onset-rime** training rather than **phoneme** level training) was actually not statistically reliable, but training in **phonological awareness** coupled with relating the training to written words did produce reliable effects. Conversely, there is now evidence that children given Reading Recovery instruction respond more rapidly if the instruction is supplemented with **phonological awareness** training (Iverson and Tunmer, 1983).

Both these lines of evidence suggest that a combination of structured reading instruction coupled with **phonological awareness** training should work particularly well for children who are struggling in the early phases of learning to read. In a now classic study in the UK, Peter Hatcher, Charles Hulme and Andrew Ellis (1994) set out to test this idea. They compared three forms of intervention for 7-year-old poor readers, **phonological awareness** training (P), reading instruction (R) or combined training in reading and **phonological awareness** (R + P), each delivered by trained teachers. The R + P programme could be seen as a kind of melding of the Reading Recovery approach (since there was a lot of book reading and teachers took a **running record** of the errors children made while reading) and the **Phonological Awareness** training approach (children were trained to identify sounds in words starting with larger segments such as syllables and **rimes**, moving onto segmenting and blending **phonemes**). The most effective intervention was the R + P integrated programme which incorporated training in **phonological awareness** and letter-sound knowledge. In addition, metacognitive exercises made explicit the links between these skills in the context of writing. Crucially, sessions also included reading from carefully selected books, of appropriate difficulty for each individual child. This work has formed the basis of a series of intervention studies conducted by our group at the University of York, including ones we describe in this book. One critical finding from this study, which is in line with findings from earlier studies, was that training in **phonological awareness** alone was effective in increasing children's phonological skills but that this did not result in reliable increases in the children's reading skills.

The Reading with Phonology Programme

Peter Hatcher's Reading with **Phonology** programme (R + P) (Hatcher, 2006) begins with an assessment of a child's reading and spelling strategies, to provide a picture of their strengths and weaknesses in tackling words that are difficult to read or write. The assessment battery includes a test of print concepts (following the methods used by Clay, in Reading Recovery), an early word recognition test comprising words frequently encountered in early reading books, and a test of letter knowledge. A key element is the '*running record*' in which the child is required to read a section of a book independently without support from the teacher (this can be as few as 20 words or a passage of between 100 and 200 words depending on level of proficiency; see Chapter 3 for details). While the child is reading, the teacher records their reading behaviours (such as errors, self-corrections, sounding out, losing the line). The record yields a reading accuracy score which is used to determine whether the text is at an easy (>94% correct), instructional (90–94% correct), or difficult (<90% correct) level for the child, and the record can be analysed to determine whether the child is using appropriate reading strategies. The child is also asked to write 'a short story' (this might be just a sentence) and then to read it aloud, and to write their name and some key words. These writing samples provide information about the child's level of written language (spelling and handwriting skills) and are analysed to assess how well they can segment sounds for spelling. More formally, they receive a comprehensive test of **phonological awareness**, *Sound Linkage* (Hatcher, 2000a), which taps awareness of syllables, rimes and **phonemes**. Performance on the test is used to determine the point at which training in phonological skills should begin and to monitor progress during the intervention.

The main elements of the *Reading with **Phonology*** teaching approach are:

- training in letter knowledge;
- teaching **concepts of print**;
- training to manipulate the sounds of words, particularly **phoneme** awareness;
- applying letter and sound knowledge to word reading and writing (**phonics**);
- reading text at an easy level (for reinforcement, practice and confidence);
- reading text at an **instructional level** (to practise decoding words in context, with teacher support); and
- writing a simple story (could be just one word or one sentence, with support).

The findings from the assessment are used to plan the first lesson which follows a set format and is delivered within an agreed time frame. Subsequently the content of the lesson is tailored to take account of the pace at which the child is learning. Lessons are individual, last for 30 minutes, and usually occur twice a week. Progression within the programme follows Clay's procedure of consolidating children's reading strengths with material that can be read with more than 94% accuracy. A second objective is working to overcome confusions and learning new skills with text that can be read with 90 to 94% accuracy. The **running record** is also used to identify the set of skills to be taught at the next level. A key skill that teachers need to develop is how to choose books at the appropriate level. In the UK, a database of books which have been graded for difficulty is available on the internet; however this frequently requires updating because books go out of print.

Modifications of the Reading with Phonology Programme

The success of the R + P programme when delivered individually to children with reading delay was a spur to future developments. In the hope of circumventing reading difficulties in 'at-risk' groups, we adapted the approach for delivery by mainstream teachers to whole classes of children in 20 schools (Hatcher, Hulme and Snowling, 2004). Schools were divided into four groups which received different forms of teaching. At the core of all four programmes teachers were taught to deliver a high quality, systematic phonically-based form of reading instruction. However, in three out of four groups, this teaching was supplemented with work on oral **phonological awareness**. This was delivered either at the level of **phonemes**, **onset/rimes** or using both **rimes** and **phonemes**.

In this mainstream approach, it is important to emphasize that children at risk of literacy problems were taught alongside their peers in whole classes over the first two years of school (5 terms in all). All children in these mixed ability groups received what we would consider high quality phonically-based reading instruction. Diary records indicated that typically the children received the phonological aspects of the work in the classroom and read to the teacher individually but there was consider-able variation in the intensity of the approach across the 20 schools that were involved. The finding for the majority of children in these classes who were learning to read normally was that they did not show any additional benefits of the phonological training. Importantly, however, the approach was helpful for children at risk of reading difficulties on school entry. For 'at-risk' children, supplementing the reading curriculum with **phoneme** awareness training during the first five terms of school slowed the decline in reading attainment (relative to their peers) that was seen in at-risk children who did not receive such training.

The findings of this study showed clearly that the R + P approach is helpful for children entering school with poorly developed oral language and phonological skills; however, its effects were small. Perhaps not surprisingly, teaching literacy skills to at-risk children alongside their mainstream peers did not enable them to keep up. Rather for these children it seems necessary to move to a more individualised approach. Furthermore, although in the original R + P approach, **phonological awareness** training followed a sequence of large to small units, in this study we had shown that training at the **phoneme** level is most effective. Accordingly we have focused on **phoneme** level training in subsequent work on reading intervention.

Delivering intervention on an individual basis is a costly process and we therefore turned to consider whether we could modify the R + P approach for delivery by trained teaching assistants. Our first step was to pilot such a pro-gramme in which the reading elements of the approach were taught on a one-to-one basis and small group work was directed to training in **phoneme** awareness, letter knowledge and linkage activities. The programme was delivered by trained teaching assistants on a daily basis (for 12 weeks) and was compared with the *UK Early Literacy Support* programme of teaching (Department for Education and Skills, 2001). The training and support of teaching assistants is regarded as fundamental to the success of reading intervention and, importantly in our view, the teaching assistants were supported fortnightly in tutorials throughout the intervention. We found that both programmes were effective for groups of 6-year-old children whose reading was developing slowly in their second year in school. In fact both programmes moved children up to being in the low average range of reading skills for their age.

We were left with the question of whether such an approach would be effective for children with more significant difficulties in learning to read. To address this issue, we conducted a **randomised controlled trial** targeting 5–6 year-old children selected for being in roughly the bottom 8% of the population for reading development (Hatcher et al., 2006). The children who participated were allocated at random to receive the intervention either for a 20-week period (20-week

Intervention group) or for a 10-week period (10-week Intervention group; these children acted as a 'waiting-list' control group for the first 10-weeks and then received the teaching during weeks 10–20). (At the beginning of the study, the 10-week Intervention group was by chance marginally better at reading than the 20-week group; these baseline differences were controlled statistically in all analyses).

The results of the study were very encouraging. After 10 weeks of daily intervention, the children in the 20-week intervention group had made significant gains on a test of single word reading ability compared to controls in the 'waiting list' group who made negligible gains. In the subsequent 10 weeks when both groups received the intervention, the 10-week Intervention group began to catch up with the 20-week group now that they were given the intervention.

But we need to ask whether this approach would prove to be effective in schools once the research team had withdrawn, that is could it be self-sustaining in the everyday context of schools? This is an important question that the local authority in which we worked were keen to address. In the year following the completion of our research, 50 teaching assistants and one teacher from 38 primary schools undertook a four-day training programme delivered by members of the local authority in six venues across the county, coordinated by Glynnis Smith, Consultant in Inclusion and Simon Gibbs, Educational Psychologist. Following training, the 'trainees' delivered the R + P programme to 142 children, the majority being children in Year 1.

Children received an average of 38 sessions in a 10-week period and the teaching assistants tested the children before and after they carried out the intervention. On average children made over 7 months progress in reading in the 10-week period. Although it is impossible to be certain that the gains were due to the programme and not a more general effect of the special attention they received, we are encouraged that the findings of this field trial replicate those of the research trials. In short, we think the results are educationally very significant and underline the efficacy (as well as cost-effectiveness) of *Reading with* **Phonology** as an early intervention for children with literacy difficulties at the end of the first year in school.

However, we need to signal a note of caution. Although we have consistently found that the average gain in reading skills as a result of the R + P intervention is good, it is important to stress that some children (between 20% to 30%) remained very poor readers. Such children clearly require ongoing support if their literacy skills are to be brought to within the average range. Moreover, children varied in their responsiveness to the teaching they received and a small number could be defined as **treatment 'non-responders'**. These children were typically those with more severe phonological impairments, poor vocabulary skills and of lower socio-economic status.

Intervention for Treatment Non-Responders

The finding of a poor response to intervention by socially disadvantaged children with relatively poor receptive vocabulary and poor **phoneme** awareness prompted us to look at these children in more detail (Duff et al., 2008). By the time of this second phase of our study, the children were aged 7:07 years and approximately 22 months had elapsed since they received the *Reading with **Phonology*** programme. In the interim, the majority of these children had not received any specific literacy support though it is difficult to validate this report because formal records were not available.

The assessment battery was exploratory and included a broad range of cognitive and linguistic measures. In addition to reading and spelling tasks, we included three **phoneme** awareness tests (segmenting, blending and deletion), and a test of letter knowledge. We assessed language skills using tests of expressive **grammar**, vocabulary (as assessed by word definitions) and phonological skills using a test of nonword repetition. We also assessed more general cognitive resources such as speed of processing, sustained and divided attention.

We found that the children had very varied profiles (see Chapter 7 for case examples); however, on average, they showed very poor language (vocabulary and **grammar**) and very poor **phoneme** awareness skills for their age. In contrast, although they showed a tendency to have problems in attention control, their speed of processing skills were broadly within the normal range. It may have been appropriate simply to have provided these children with a further course of '*Reading with **Phonology*'*, perhaps delivered more intensively on an individual basis. But instead, we felt it appropriate to design and pilot an intervention that would take account of the fact that these children had significant oral language impairments. If it is the case, as we believe, that oral language and particularly vocabulary development are foundations for the development of **phonological awareness**, then boosting children's vocabulary and fostering wider oral language proficiency should benefit the development of their **phonological awareness**.

Accordingly, we developed an integrated programme of reading, **phonological awareness** and vocabulary training which we nicknamed *REVI (Reading with Vocabulary Intervention)*. REVI was designed as a 9-week programme for delivery on a one-to-one basis by teaching assistants to children with poor reading in the context of poor oral language and incorporates the basic elements of the R + P programme described above. To take account of the attentional problems of the children and the likely benefits of distributed practice, daily instruction was divided into two 15-minute sessions. We describe this programme in detail in Chapter 7. For present purposes we outline only the essential features of the approach.

The first session of REVI began with five minutes of reading; the books we used were the springboard for a subsequent five minutes of vocabulary instruction in which the teaching assistant first contextualised the word showing how it related to the book, explained its meaning and gave the child examples of the word in other contexts. The child's role was to repeat the target word several times to assist in securing its pronunciation, and to engage with the word's meaning by generating examples of its use in different contexts. This procedure derives from the assumption that the simple vocabulary in the texts that poor readers are able to read is too limited to boost vocabulary development and hence, sophisticated words have to

Figure 2.2 Illustration of a picture sequence used for the narrative task (based on materials from Black Sheep Press)

be taught to such children in a rich and multi-contextual manner (Beck, Perfetti and McKeown, 1982).

The last five minutes of the session were spent on a **narrative** writing task. The children used a sequence of pictures as prompts from which to tell a story (see Figure 2.2). Following some oral work on the quality of the language, the teaching assistant encouraged the child to write down a small part of the story.

The second session each day involved a modification of the R + P programme. The first three minutes were spent revising the target vocabulary taught in the earlier session. There was then five minutes of **phonological awareness** training involving segmenting, blending and deletion of initial, medial and final **phonemes**, followed by three minutes dedicated to teaching of **sight words** through multi-sensory activities. After this, the teaching assistant introduced the child to a new book at the **instructional level** of reading, using this time to discuss concepts about print. The child also had an opportunity to link their emerging phonological and **sight word** skills to reading when reading the book with the teaching assistant and then alone (3 minutes). The session finished with revision and reinforcement of the day's target vocabulary and **sight words** (1 minute). Every fifth day of the intervention was designated as a consolidation day.

Twelve children defined as 'treatment non-responders' were recipients of the intervention. At the time of its delivery, the children were aged 8 years, and their reading skills fell roughly within the bottom 7% of the population. In the absence of a control group, it was important that we had been able to monitor the progress of these children over a baseline period during which time they made no statistically significant gains in the reading, **phonological awareness** or oral language abilities that we measured. In contrast, by the end of the intervention they had made significant gains in word reading, letter-sound knowledge, **phoneme** seg-mentation, and expressive **grammar**. In addition, by the end of the intervention, the children were significantly better at defining words that they had been taught than those they had not. Children failed to make any significant progress on the measures during the baseline period in contrast to the demonstrable progress made during the intervention period. We revisited the children some six months after the intervention ceased to monitor maintenance of gains. Gains made in **phoneme** awareness and in vocabulary were maintained and reading raw scores increased significantly in the maintenance period.

A WAY FORWARD? EARLY INTERVENTION AT THE FOUNDATION OF LITERACY SKILLS

The studies considered here show that interventions can be effective but at the same time, they confirm that there is generally a minority of children who fail to respond (Fuchs and Fuchs, 2002). Although the evidence-base is thin, clinical experience suggests that these non-responders include a high proportion of children with oral language difficulties that come to school ill-prepared to develop literacy. Such children arguably should be given the intervention as soon as they enter school. Logically, there are two different ways to support their language needs with a view to safe-guarding their literacy development. The first is what might be called the direct approach – that is to provide these children with an intervention that targets the development of pre-literacy and literacy skills. The second is an indirect approach. This approach takes as its starting point the finding that oral language is the foundation of phoneme awareness, and a better predictor of reading development in children from high-risk groups than **phonological awareness**. Within this view, children who enter school with poor speech and language should receive training in oral language skills (particularly vocabulary) because this will foster the development of metalinguistic skills including **phoneme** awareness. The latter approach should also be more helpful than the former for the development of reading comprehension.

Based on this theoretical rationale, we went on to compare two different intervention programmes designed to promote foundation literacy skills in children during their first school year: a ***Phonology** with Reading* intervention (P + R; so named to highlight the fact that the programme was designed for non-readers) and an *Oral Language* intervention (OL). The remainder of this book is concerned with variants of these two intervention programmes.

SUMMING UP: THE EFFECTS OF READING AND LANGUAGE INTERVENTIONS FOR POOR READERS

We have summarised the methods and results from an array of studies examining the effectiveness of interventions to boost the reading and phonological skills of children in the early school years. The studies have differed both in the populations of children included, and in the rigour of the designs used. Nevertheless, some consistent results have emerged. It seems that interventions that target reading and **phonological awareness** in a unified way (the R + P programme of the original Hatcher, Hulme and Ellis study, and later variants of this programme) are effective in boosting the reading skills of children who are struggling in the early stages of learning to read. When this approach was extended to mainstream classes (rather than being exclusively delivered to children with reading problems), the results suggested that additional phonological training was not really important for typically developing children; such children learned to read just as well without it provided they received systematic **phonics**-based teaching. But for children at risk of reading problems, additional oral phonological training, particularly training focusing on **phonemes**, was important. Finally, we showed in a preliminary way that training broader oral language skills (vocabulary and **narrative** speaking skills) is certainly possible, and this spurred us on to the Nuffield trial which is described in Chapters 4, 5, 6 and 8 of this book.

We hope this chapter demonstrates that it is quite possible to collect rigorous evidence for the effectiveness of interventions, and that it is important to put our ideas for educational practice on a firm footing that is evidence-based.

Chapter 3

Principles of Intervention: Screening, Assessment and Monitoring Progress

The term 'assessment' means different things to different people. Researchers make use of formal assessments to evaluate the efficacy of interventions; teachers make use of assessments to monitor how well a class of children are progressing and to identify children in need of support; specialist practitioners use assessments to 'diagnose' learning difficulties and to devise individualised intervention programmes. In this chapter we will see that assessment in all its forms (screening, diagnostic testing and monitoring) plays a key role in any successful intervention. In the first place, screening can provide an indication of which children are 'at risk' and who would benefit from further support. Next, a more detailed individual assessment can provide a clear indication of a child's *strengths* and *weaknesses*, about the strategies they use and also what they know. This information is useful for specifying which skills should be targeted within an intervention, and it can also tell us about the *severity* of a child's difficulties – how far the child is lagging behind his or her peers. In turn, this can help determine what level of support should be provided. Finally, assessments can be used to monitor progress. Such assessments are important because they tell us whether a child is responding to an intervention – are they making the expected rate of progress? Is the intervention effective, should it be continued or is it necessary to change tactics?

Since assessment can serve different purposes, it is not surprising that there are different ways in which assessments are formulated. In this chapter we provide an explanation of the different types of assessment that exist and the ways in which these different types of assessment can be useful. We will focus on three types of assessment: classroom screening to select a child for intervention; formal testing

Developing Language and Literacy: Effective Intervention in the Early Years
By Julia M. Carroll, Claudine Bowyer-Crane, Fiona J. Duff, Charles Hulme, and Margaret J. Snowling
© 2011 John Wiley & Sons, Ltd

that should occur before and after an intervention; and monitoring which is less formal and forms an ongoing part of the intervention.

THE ASSESSMENT PROCESS

The role of assessment is illustrated in Figure 3.1. As the figure illustrates, we believe that assessment forms a crucial part of good teaching practice for all children, but especially for children with special educational needs.

- *Regular screening* helps to identify children who may be struggling to keep up. Screening normally involves a brief assessment of a whole class of children.
- Following screening, children identified as showing slow progress can be given more *detailed assessment* of their strengths and weaknesses. Such 'diagnostic' assessment helps to decide which children would benefit from *intervention* and how the intervention can be adapted to suit an individual child's needs (this is discussed in more detail in Chapter 7).
- During the intervention, *regular monitoring* would be carried out to see how well a child is responding to the teaching they are receiving. If they are not responding it is important to consider how the intervention could be changed to suit them better.
- After a certain period of time has elapsed (say three, six or twelve months), more *formal reassessment* on the same measures as those used before the intervention will provide clear and objective evidence of a child's progress.

In this way, assessment informs intervention, allowing more effective tuition and hopefully better progress. Over time, the aim is that performance in the assessment will improve to the targeted level so that intervention can cease.

Screening Measures

Typically a teacher would use a range of screening measures regularly to help select children who might benefit from additional support. An example of the use of

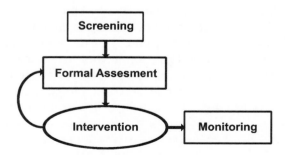

Figure 3.1   The assessment cycle

There are six phonic phases which, in brief, comprise:

1 Distinguish between different sounds in environment; show awareness of rhyme and alliteration; blend and segment orally

2 Know about 19 letter sound correspondences. Blend and segment VC and CVC (two and three letter) words; know some tricky words

3 Know one way of representing each of 42 **phonemes**. Blend and segment CVC words including graphemes of more than one letter and two syllable words. Read and spell tricky words

4 Blend adjacent consonants in words and apply when reading unfamiliar texts. Segment adjacent consonants and apply to spelling

5 Know alternative ways of spelling/pronouncing graphemes. Spell complex words using phonically plausible attempts

6 Apply phonic skills and knowledge with increasing fluency when reading unfamiliar words in texts. Recognise and spell increasing number of complex words including applying rules for adding prefixes and suffixes.

Box 3.1 The six phonic phases

screening as a first step to intervention comes from the 'Phonic Phases' used in the *Letters and Sounds* programme that is recommended in English schools at the time of writing. The phases are qualitative descriptions of a child's knowledge and skills in **phonics** as they progress through the early years of literacy instruction. Descriptors of the Phases are shown in Box 3.1.

Teachers who use the *Letter and Sounds* programme are encouraged to assess the phase that each child has achieved regularly, say after each half-term. A child who is not progressing through the phases as quickly as other children would be a potential candidate for intervention.

We know that the phases are a very good proxy measure for a child's reading skill. When collecting national norms for the *York Assessment of Reading Comprehension* (YARC), the authors asked teachers in the schools which were using the *Letters and Sounds* programme to provide data on the phonic phase achieved by each of the children who were tested. There was a high degree of agreement (correlation) between a child's phase as rated by their teacher and their scores on the detailed literacy assessments that were carried out. Therefore we are confident that teacher's judgements about how well the children in their class are learning **phonics** are valid and reliable. It follows that these judgements can be thought of as a kind of screening to identify children who are progressing slowly. This brief screening process can then form the starting point for more detailed assessment.

Assessment Before and After Intervention

We would expect any intervention to begin with a range of assessments, and we would also expect that at least some of these assessments would be repeated after the child has received intervention for a specified amount of time. However, it can be difficult to know which assessments are most important to include.

Many measures of progress in teaching, including progress through the Phonic Phases, are *criterion referenced*. **Criterion referenced** literacy tests give lists of key skills, or, more simply, lists of words or letters that children may know at a particular stage of development. Such measures are not standardised and there are no population norms. Rather, there is a list of criteria in a given domain and achievement is monitored against these criteria. For example, within the Early Years Foundation Stage, there is a list of criteria for reading-related skills that a child might show during their first year of school. These include:

Knows that, in English, print is read from left to right and from top to bottom.

Reads a range of familiar and common words and simple sentences independently.

Teachers are asked to record whether a child fulfils these criteria at the end of their reception year. It is not the focus of these assessments to determine whether a child is average or below average for their age, but to know whether they have specific skills or not. This is *criterion referenced* measurement. **Criterion referenced tests** are particularly important for *planning* an intervention. In order to decide which elements to include in an intervention, it is important to know whether a child knows a particular letter or word, and hence whether it is useful to teach these things.

In contrast to **criterion referenced tests**, *norm referenced* tests compare a child's performance to the *average* for their age. Such tests are generally designed to test across a wide age range. For example, the *York Assessment of Reading for Comprehension (Primary)* is aimed at 5- to 11-year-old children and provides information about whether a child is average, above average or below average for their age in terms of their reading accuracy, reading speed and reading comprehension. However, although performance on the test can be analysed qualitatively to assess the child's use of reading strategies, it does not give information about whether the child has particular skills or pieces of knowledge.

Norm referenced tests are particularly important in assessing children's *progress* over time. If an intervention carries on for six months, for example, it is likely that over this time a child will show progress in reading. However, if we only use a **criterion referenced test**, it is difficult to know whether this progress is more or less than we would expect over the six month period. **Norm referenced** tests help us see whether, in comparison to his or her peers, a child is catching up or falling behind over the period of the intervention.

A Word About Test Scores

One of the tricky issues to be faced when using a norm-referenced test is how to interpret test scores. Most **norm referenced** tests provide one or more of the following scores: *age equivalent scores*, **standard scores** or **percentile scores**. *Age equivalent scores* indicate the age level at which a child is working. An age equivalent of 6 year 3 months indicates that a child is working at the level expected of an average child of that age. On first glance, these seem like an easy score to interpret and it is therefore not surprising that teachers (and parents) like to speak of 'age equivalents'. However, age equivalents are extremely *difficult to interpret*, and if interpreted literally they can be very misleading for reasons that we will now explain.

Although seemingly transparent, it is difficult to use an age equivalent score to know how impaired a child is *in comparison to their peers in the same age group*. This is because the rate of change in reading skills differs across the age range and a given 'lag' means different things at different stages. To illustrate, a delay of two years in age equivalent terms is quite serious in a seven year old child because it means that they have barely started to read (they are reading 'like' a 5-year-old). However, in a fifteen year old, the same 'lag' of two years would represent a relatively minor impairment because reading skills are developing less quickly in older children and hence there is less of a difference between the reading skills of a 13- and a 15-year-old. A further limitation of age equivalent scores is that they are relatively insensitive to small changes – often age equivalents will be given at only six month intervals, meaning that many improvements will not be reflected in changes in the age equivalent score.

Standard scores deal with these two problems because they are calculated separately for different age groups. A child who is reading at the average level for their age will achieve a standard score of 100. A score of 85 indicates a moderate level of difficulty (around 16% of children would score at this level or below). Since these scores are standardised across ages, it is easy to compare them for children of different ages, and to see which has the most severe impairment. Most crucially, they can be used to compare the same child at different stages, or to see whether a child is improving more or less than would be expected in a given time.

Percentile scores rank a child's score in comparison to other children of the same age. A score at the 30th percentile indicates that 30% of the population would score *worse* than this. **Percentile scores** are useful for expressing a child's position relative to other children, but they have some disadvantages. They tend to magnify differences in the middle of the range – **percentile scores** of 35 versus 65 sound very different, though in fact they are both well within the average range. In contrast, **percentile scores** minimise differences at the extremes of the range – **percentile scores** of 2 and 9 sound quite similar but they indicate very different levels of functioning (approximately equivalent in standard score terms to 70 and 80).

For all of these reasons, we recommend using **standard scores** to assess children whenever possible.

How Specific Should a Test Be?

When assessing skills, some measures are very specific, while others are very wide ranging. For example, a letter knowledge test assesses a very specific skill, while a listening comprehension test will involve a wide range of skills. Generally speaking, specific measures that are closely related to the skill you wish to improve are probably the best ways to monitor growth in that skill. For example, if you are teaching vocabulary, it is better to test improvement using a list of the words you have covered rather than a standardised vocabulary test. On the other hand, broader tests are useful for examining *generalisation* of the skills you have taught. For example, the ultimate aim of teaching letter knowledge and training **phoneme** awareness is to improve reading and spelling. Therefore it is useful to include a reading and spelling measure because improving these skills is the objective of the exercise.

In the following section, we consider different language and literacy skills and provide some recommendations for tests to use for assessment.

LANGUAGE AND LITERACY SKILLS

Word Reading

Tests of word reading are relatively easy to administer and there are plenty of them about. These tests are both **criterion referenced** and **norm referenced**. For example, it is typical for curricula to provide list of key words that children should know.

Norm referenced tests of word reading are often included in larger batteries of reading measures such as the *York Assessment of Reading for Comprehension*, the *Wide Range Achievement Test* or the *Wechsler Individual Achievement Test*. There are also some freely available word reading tests, such as the *Burt Word Reading Test*, but care should be taken to ensure the test provides complete **standard scores** (the Burt, for example, provides only age equivalent scores, which as described above can be very difficult to interpret).

Norm referenced tests normally include a range of words that can be read by sight as well as words that can be decoded. A **norm referenced** test will allow you to decide how severely impaired a child's reading is given their age. Moreover, because reading is likely to be one of the key skills that you hope to improve during an intervention, a **norm referenced** test will be helpful for monitoring progress. In addition, a list of key words is a useful tool for planning which **sight words** should be included in training.

Text Reading

The ultimate aim of language and literacy interventions is to ensure that a child can read passages of text with understanding and enjoyment, and therefore it seems obvious that measuring text reading should form part of the assessment. We recommend regular monitoring of text reading using a ***running record***, which is described in more detail in the monitoring section below. A **running record** provides an estimate of the child's reading ability, but not a comparison to other children of the same age; it is not a **norm referenced** measure.

Some measures of reading are suitable for administration to groups. These are often based on sentence completion: children are asked to read a sentence and select a word that fits within the sentence. For example, the *Suffolk Reading Scale* and the *Group Reading Test* fit within this format. Although these tests are a quick and useful way to screen for reading difficulties, it is difficult to know whether a child has difficulties in reading words correctly or difficulties in understanding the sentence, or both. For this reason, we advise using measures that assess reading accuracy and reading comprehension separately. The *Salford Sentence Reading Test,* for example, is a measure which measures sentence reading accuracy, and therefore could be used as a measure of text reading. There are also tests which provide scores for both text reading accuracy and comprehension in the same measure, described below.

Reading Comprehension

As well as assessing children's accuracy of text reading, it is crucial to know whether they understand what they have read. National attainment tests usually include a measure of reading comprehension in which children are scored as meeting or not meeting several level descriptors. Such a **criterion referenced test** is useful for knowing which particular skills a child has or lacks. However, it is not very useful for measuring progress after a short-term reading intervention because it lacks sensitivity over short periods of time, and provides no direct estimate of how far behind a child is for their age.

We therefore advise the additional use of **norm referenced** tests to assess reading comprehension. There are several measures available, many of which will give separate scores for text reading accuracy and reading comprehension. For example, the *York Assessment of Reading for Comprehension(YARC)* and the *Neale Analysis of Reading Abilities II (NARA II)* are both measures in which children are asked to read a passage and answer questions on that passage. Of course, for children in the earliest stages of school, a reading comprehension test may not be appropriate. If a child is reading only a few words, there is little point in using a reading comprehension measure. However, measures are available from a word reading age of 5 or 6 years old, so once a child can happily read a few simple sentences, it is possible to assess this skill.

Letter Knowledge

Letter knowledge is a key skill in early literacy, and we would always recommend assessing letter knowledge when planning an intervention. However, in this case, a **norm referenced** test is not essential, for a few reasons. The first is that typically developing children normally know the majority of their letters by the end of their first year in school, and so there is not much age-related variation in this measure. It is therefore not difficult to make a judgement about how far behind a child is in their letter knowledge compared to other children of the same age. Second, it is easy to test a child's knowledge of every letter, whereas it is not possible to test a child's knowledge of every word. A **criterion referenced test** of letter knowledge is therefore both easy to create and reliable; it is normally sufficient to ask children to give the names and sounds when shown the 26 letters and some additional digraphs (such as '*ch*', '*sh*' or '*th*'). Finally, knowing which letters a child does or does not know is a key element in planning the intervention.

Phonological Awareness

In terms of assessing phonological awareness, both norm referenced and **criterion referenced tests** are useful. Again, it is vital to have an understanding of what a child can and cannot do to allow effective planning of an intervention. However, it is also useful to have a measure of growth in this skill over time, and to have an understanding of how severe the child's difficulty is in this area. In turn, this information will ensure that an appropriate amount of time is given to training phonemic skills.

Earlier, we discussed the 'Phonic Phases' which form part of the Letters and Sounds programme. These are an excellent example of **criterion referenced** measures. For example, in Phase Four, children 'can blend adjacent consonants in words and apply this skill when reading unfamiliar texts'. This type of information is essential for planning an intervention, but it is also useful to have **norm referenced** measures to provide an indication of severity of a child's difficulties. **Norm referenced** measures of phonological awareness include the *Comprehensive Test of Phonological Processing*, the *Phonological Abilities Test*, the *Preschool and Primary Inventory of Phonological Awareness* and the *YARC Early Reading Test*.

Vocabulary

Though there are **norm referenced** vocabulary tests, we suggest it might be more useful to use a **criterion referenced** measure for monitoring the impact of an intervention. Knowledge of word meanings is item-specific, and highly dependent upon an individual's experience: two children might have a similar level of intelligence, a similar level of reading, and a similar level of general language skill, but will differ in the specific words they are able to understand and use. In addition, some words are very important for understanding instruction and information in the classroom (such as 'why', 'how', 'more' and 'less'), and so it is important to know whether children understand these particular words.

Word knowledge can be tested in three ways: whether the child understands the word (e.g., given a number of options, can they point to the right picture that represents the word's meaning?), whether the child can use the word appropriately (e.g., can the child name a picture that represents the word, or put the word in a meaningful sentence?), and whether the child can provide a definition of the word (a good definition might be to give an alternative word that shares the same meaning – a synonym, or a definition from which you can deduce the target word). Before beginning your intervention, compile a list of words that you are going to teach the child. These may be key words, like the examples above, or words that are used in the topic the class have been working on. Test their knowledge of these words at the beginning of your intervention, and again at the end. Remember that knowing a word in terms of understanding it does not mean the same as knowing how to use or explain a word. It is therefore useful to test both forms of knowledge.

You may wish in addition to use **norm referenced** tests. For understanding a word's meaning the *British Picture Vocabulary Scale III* is a simple to administer test; children are asked to select which one of four pictures best illustrates a given word. A test of naming can give some indication of a child's ability to access words from long-term memory. **Norm referenced** measures of picture naming are often included within broader measures of language or general intellectual development, as are measures of the ability to define words. Such tests are usually administered by speech and language therapists or educational psychologists.

Listening Comprehension

It is not easy to measure linguistic comprehension, because understanding what we hear involves many different component skills. At present there are, to our knowledge, no well-standardised tests of listening comprehension suitable for administration by non-specialist teachers. We therefore recommend using criterion reference tests. In devising or choosing a test, it is critical that it matches the aim of intervention: are you meaningfully testing an aspect of listening comprehension that you are explicitly targeting during your intervention work? For example, if you are working with a child who has difficulty following instructions, this may be the skill you wish to test. With a number of props, you can simply build up instructions for the child which vary in the amount of key information they carry:

- *Put the car on the box.*
- *Put the red car on the green box.*
- *Put the red car on the green box behind the blue lorry.*

You must be sure to check before testing that the child understands the key vocabulary that your test uses – here, colours and vehicles – so that you are truly testing listening and not vocabulary knowledge (a child might fail because they don't know red from green, rather than because they couldn't attend well to the linguistic information).

For a test that assesses the ability to integrate the meanings of words and sentences across extended lengths of language or discourse, you could read aloud short stories to the child and subsequently ask them questions about the story. At a basic level, your questions can be factual, for example after telling a story about a red bus, you could simply ask the child the colour of the bus. If you have targeted higher level language skills in your intervention (e.g., inferencing – using information to make predictions and links), your questions would need to test these skills (e.g., in a story about a girl who goes out to play in her wellies you could ask the child what the weather was like – even if the story doesn't explicitly say it had been raining). The key is to identify the skill or skills you are trying to assess and make sure that your measure is tapping those skills.

Narrative Skills

Narrative skills refer to a child's ability to tell a story or describe events in a comprehensible way. Both **criterion referenced** and **norm referenced** tests are useful for assessing **narrative** skills. It is very easy to construct your own **criterion referenced narrative** task by selecting a series of engaging pictures that tell a story and leave open plenty of room for children to use their imagination to go beyond the pictures. However, a few important points must be noted. The number of pictures and the themes that they convey must be suited to the child's learning and language levels. Also, you must be clear on what aspects of language you are trying to measure via this task.

   We suggest you use the scoring guidelines from the Nuffield Oral Language Intervention as a start point for your assessment of **narrative** skills. There may be other aspects of language that you will be targeting in your intervention, and you will need to make sure that your story picture sequence, or your instructions, will bring these features out in the child's speech (e.g., if you want to monitor a child's use of the past tense it may be necessary to ask the child to tell a story as though it happened a very long time ago). If you are using the **narrative** task as a tool for targeting content and form of children's language then the *Renfrew Action Picture Test* can be used, which assesses the information and **grammar** in children's speech. We would also recommend the *Renfrew Bus Story, The Squirrel Story* or *Peter and the Cat* (both from Black Sheep Press). Table 3.1 provides a summary of the kinds of tests that could be used to provide a comprehensive assessment of early language and literacy skills. A list of test references is in Appendix 3.1.

MONITORING PROGRESS DURING THE INTERVENTION

As we have seen, effective teaching depends on effective assessment and monitoring. Assessment allows you to plan teaching sessions that are at the right level for the children, and it helps you see whether the teaching is working. In particular, assessment allows you to pinpoint the particular types of mistakes a child is making and to reflect on what this shows about their underlying thought

Table 3.1   Basic tests to provide a comprehensive assessment of language and literacy skills

Skill	Use norm referenced or criterion referenced?	Examples of useful measures
Word Reading	Both	• YARC Early Reading • National Curriculum key **sight word**s
Reading Comprehension	Norm referenced	• YARC Passage Reading
Letter Knowledge	**Criterion referenced**	• All the letters in random order
Phonological Awareness	Both	• Phonic Phases • Comprehensive Test of Phonological Processing • YARC Early Reading
Vocabulary	Both	• British Picture Vocabulary Scale 3
Listening comprehension	**Criterion referenced**	
Speaking and **narrative** skills	Both	• Renfrew Action Picture Test • Renfrew Bus Story

processes. This process is known as ***formative assessment*** or *assessment for learning*.

There are several different ways in which assessment for learning forms part of our intervention programmes. We give two detailed examples below: the **running record** and the **narrative** task.

Taking a Running Record

One of the key ways in which to keep track of reading progress is the system of book levels and '**running records**' created by Marie Clay (Clay, 1985) and developed by Peter Hatcher in his Reading Intervention programme. We used this system as part of the **Phonology** with Reading programme and as part of the Reading with Vocabulary (REVI) Intervention.

The reading system which forms part of each of the reading interventions consists of a large number of books. These have now been classified according to finely-graded book reading levels (see http://www.cumbria.gov.uk/childrensservices/reading/books/viewlist.asp). The grading system takes account of how many words there are in the book, how many longer words there are, how long the sentences used are, and how complex the grammar in the book is. The grading provides a sensitive measure of how complex the book will be to read, standardised across many different reading schemes.

Within the Reading Intervention framework, a distinction is made between books that can be read by a child with at least 95% accuracy (*easy level book*), and books that are read with between 90–94% accuracy (*instructional level book*). A child's accuracy level is determined by the TA taking a ***running record***. There are four types of reading activity:

1   *Reading at the easy level*: A reading session begins with the children reading an easy-level book (a book they can read independently). This practice ensures that children begin the intervention sessions with a successful and positive learning experience.
2   *Reading at the **instructional level***: Children are then required to read a book at their **instructional level**, with minimal help from the teacher. An '**instructional level**' book is a book that was introduced at the end of the previous teaching session. If the child is in the very early stages of learning to read, it may be better to use a sentence written by the teacher or a caption book. During this activity, the teacher takes a **running record** (described in Box 3.2). At its most basic level, this involves recording the success or otherwise of every word that the child attempts to read. A child's reading accuracy is then calculated.

1   Plan the text that you will use for the **running record**. For shorter books, this will include the whole book. If longer books are being read, use a section of up to around 100 words.

2   Using the **running record** form, or any piece of paper, note the child's response to each word:
    a. If the word is correct, give a tick
    b. If the word is incorrect, give a cross
    c. If the child inserts a word, give an arrow
    d. At the end of each page, draw a line under the ticks (this helps to keep your place)
3   After the reading session, work out the percentage of words the child has read correctly using the following calculation: (words read correctly)/(total words in the passage) × 100. This calculation is printed on the **running record** form. This will give a number between 1 and 100. Text read with less than 90% accuracy is hard, text read with 90–94% accuracy is at the **instructional level**, and text read at 95% accuracy or greater is easy.

4   If you want to record more information about the child's reading, you can use additional symbols for the errors made: for example, use T to represent that you told the child the word; use a dash to represent a word missed out; write down an incorrect word that they said; or write SC for a word they self-corrected.

A **running record** is a really useful tool in monitoring the reading skills of all children, not just children with reading difficulties. It is really helpful in deciding whether a child is reading books at the appropriate level.

Box 3.2   Taking a running record

3   *Introduction to a new book:* Each day, a child is also introduced to a new book, again at their **instructional level**. This book is selected on the basis of their reading accuracy level (calculated from the **running record**). If a child's reading accuracy is between 90–94%, new books that are introduced will be selected from the same reading level as before. Once the child has read three books with greater than 94% accuracy, new books will be selected from the next highest reading level.

Whereas in activity 2 children were required to read a book they had seen before with minimal help, much more assistance is provided when they attempt to read a

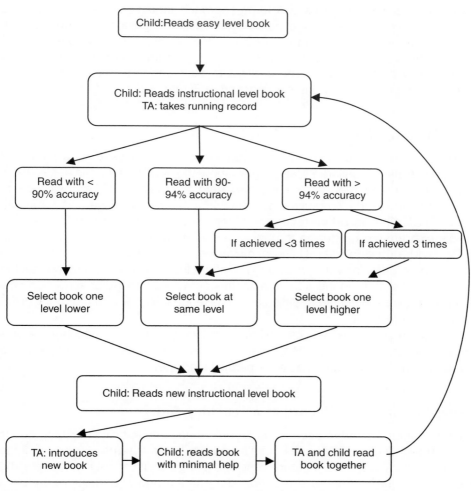

Figure 3.2   Assessing children's reading levels in order to establish appropriate books for them to read

new book. Having selected a book from the appropriate **instructional level**, the teacher first introduces it to the child by drawing attention to the title, author, plot, characters and any words that the child may find tricky to read. The child is then asked to read the book with limited help from the teacher. However, whenever the child struggles with a word, they are to be encouraged with a variety of strategies:

- sounding out the letters, then blending them together (sound linkage);
- making a good guess based on the initial letter and visual similarity with other words; and
- using context and picture cues.

Finally, the child re-reads the story along with the teacher (shared reading) to encourage fluent reading. A **scaffolding** approach should be taken here, with the teacher staying one step behind the children when they get to tricky words to give them the chance to work out the words by themselves. This new book will then become the reading book that is assessed using the **running record** (activity 2) in the next day of intervention. The process surrounding the assessment of book levels for an individual child is summarised in Figure 3.2.

The Narrative Task

In the Oral Language Intervention, a **narrative** record is used as a means of regularly assessing children's language without the need for a formal assessment (see Box 3.3). The informality of the **narrative** task puts a child at their ease to enable them to produce results that reflect their natural language and communication skills. The **narrative** record provides an opportunity for you to assess a child's **expressive language** through a story-telling activity; a task with which many children are familiar. Using a **narrative** activity such as this will help to encourage children's oral fluency and provide a foundation for writing connected text. Carried out on an individual basis, this activity is straightforward, relatively quick and can be adjusted in difficulty to challenge children with higher levels of language proficiency.

For more able children you can extend this activity by introducing longer sequences of pictures or pictures depicting more complex events, for example those involving more than one character or parallel storylines.

Using the Narrative Record as a Teaching Aid

Based on your **narrative** assessment, you can identify specific teaching points that you feel would improve the child's **expressive language**. These teaching points can be followed up in future sessions using activities that involve retelling the story and/or writing the story depending on the age and ability of the child (see Box 3.4 and Chapter 6). You may want to work on the story over a number of sessions before carrying out another assessment and moving on to new teaching

1   Select a sequence of pictures that tell a coherent story. You can use any short picture book for this activity or you can purchase resources from companies such as Black Sheep Press.

2   Place the picture story or book on the table in front of the child and ask them to look carefully at the pictures.

3   Explain to the child that you want them to tell you a story from the pictures. Emphasise that you have not seen the pictures and that you need them to explain the story to you really clearly.

4   When they are ready, ask the child to tell you the story out loud, and record the story word for word. For older children you might only want to record a short section of the story and/or use a voice recorder to ensure you get an accurate recording.

5   If the child has difficulty starting the story you can use prompts such as, 'What is happening in the first picture?' to get them started.

6   As they tell the story, give non-specific prompts to encourage the child such as, 'Mmm, yes. . .' etc. *Remember not to give specific help at this point.* If the child has difficulty moving on from picture to picture you can guide them by asking, 'What is happening in the next picture' and, 'What is happening in this picture?' (pointing at appropriate picture).

7   Read or play the story back to the child and congratulate them on being a good story teller.

8   You can then analyse the story by completing the **narrative** task record sheet shown in Appendix 8.9. Much of this analysis is qualitative in nature and will give you an indication of relative areas of strengths and weaknesses in the child's **expressive language**.

Box 3.3   How to take a narrative record

points. However, we would recommend that you carry out a new assessment each week.

General Record Keeping

In addition to the monitoring discussed above, it is also useful to chart a child's ability in each key area. We suggest using a planning and record form for each teaching session. On each form note what you plan to cover and then following the session, note how the child responded to the work covered. An example from the **Phonology** and Reading programme is shown in Table 3.2. This provides an example of how to keep track of progress in segmenting and blending. The simple record here can help you to see at a glance what types of words each child would be able to segment and blend.

Writing

- Select an appropriate (achievable) amount of the story for the child to write. This may vary from filling in a blank that represents one word in a sentence to writing a number of sentences, which may target a specific spelling pattern.
- Encourage the child to achieve as much as this task as possible without help
- Allow the child to practise first on scrap paper before writing it in his or her story book to ensure that the final product is work they can be proud of.
- Encourage sound linkage when attempting to write unknown words.
- Reinforce correct pencil grip and letter formation and use of punctuation etc.

Retelling

- With the story pictures in view of the child, read his complete story to him
- Praise him for his attempt and say that you're going to think about how together you can make it 'even better'.
- Work on a few critical points. These may concern the quality of language (e.g. correct use of the past tense; including more descriptive words etc.) or **narrative** skills (e.g. story sequence of beginning, middle and end; use of a variety of connective words etc.).

Box 3.4   Writing and retelling a narrative

CONCLUSIONS

In summary, we have shown in this chapter that assessment is a vital part of teaching generally and of intervention in particular. We have described three types of assessment: screening, formal testing and monitoring. Effective screening helps

Table 3.2   Monitoring phonological awareness: on a regular basis, the TA marks the level of segmenting/blending of which the child is capable

Child's name	Syllables	2 phoneme words	CVC words	Words with initial consonant blends	Words with final consonant blends
Segmenting Blending					

to select the right children for extra support. Detailed formal testing provides clear evidence as to a child's strengths and weaknesses to allow tailoring of an intervention, and it provides evidence as to how effective an intervention has been. Finally, monitoring should form an everyday part of an intervention, providing a brief, immediate picture of how well a child is progressing. All three elements are needed for effective ongoing support of children with difficulties.

Chapter 4

The Nuffield Language for Reading Study

Given the evidence that we discussed in Chapter 1, there is a strong case to be made for the inclusion of activities that foster good speaking and listening skills in pre-school and early school settings. Spoken language skills are the foundation for learning to read and good teaching harnesses these resources in the service of literacy development. But what of children who come to school a long way behind their peers in their speaking and listening abilities, either because they have had less exposure to spoken English than other children, or because they have a difficulty such as Specific Language Impairment? This chapter describes two language programmes we designed to help such children to develop a better foundation for learning to read. Our research involved a **randomised controlled trial** comparing the two forms of intervention and produced some encouraging findings which are ripe for translation into practice. The study shows that it is possible to improve children's vocabulary and grammatical skills and that it is also possible to produce gains in reading and spelling skills.

MOTIVATION FOR THE INTERVENTION PROGRAMMES

The aim of our study was to develop and evaluate the efficacy of two early intervention programmes to promote the language skills that underlie reading development. In thinking about the content of these programmes, we were guided by previous research findings. As we saw in chapter 2, there have now been a

Developing Language and Literacy: Effective Intervention in the Early Years
By Julia M. Carroll, Claudine Bowyer-Crane, Fiona J. Duff, Charles Hulme, and Margaret J. Snowling
© 2011 John Wiley & Sons, Ltd

number of studies which show that poor readers make significant gains in progress when they receive training in letter-sound knowledge, **phoneme** awareness and reading activities that explicitly link the letter patterns in printed words to the sound structure of those words. However the children with whom we wanted to work were younger than those included in the previous studies. It was therefore necessary to design a 'downward extension' of the programme that would be suitable for children in the very early stages of reading instruction. We described this programme as '**Phonology** with Reading' (P + R) to reflect the fact that the emphasis was to be on developing alphabetic competence, rather than reading. The main aim of the P + R programme was to foster basic reading and spelling skills. The second intervention aimed to boost oral language skills, rather than reading. We reasoned that such skills would contribute to the development of reading fluency and strengthen the foundations of reading comprehension. The 'Oral language' Programme (OL) incorporated four key elements; vocabulary training, **narrative** work, independent speaking and listening skills, and drew upon research evidence and accepted good practice.

HYPOTHESES OF THE STUDY

Given the distinct content of the two intervention programmes, we predicted that they would have differential effects. We expected the P + R programme to encourage the development of letter knowledge and **phoneme** awareness. In contrast, we expected that the OL programme to aid in the development of oral language skills including vocabulary, **narrative** and **grammar**. Of course, we knew that all of the children in the intervention would be receiving teaching in these various skills in the classroom. However, we wanted to know whether children struggling to acquire such skills could be helped by targeted work, over and above the usual 'diet' provided by the mainstream curriculum.

We hoped that the training would lead to gains in the taught skills, and also generalise to things that had not been directly taught. We therefore tested some further predictions; we predicted that training in the P + R programme would generalise to gains in decoding ability and that training in the OL programme would generalise to gains in reading comprehension. However, given that reading comprehension is heavily dependent on decoding at an early stage of reading development, we predicted that the effects of OL training on reading comprehension would be weaker than the effects of the P + R programme on decoding.

HOW DID WE SELECT CHILDREN?

We began by contacting schools in our area and telling them about the research. As a result of initial meetings with head teachers, 23 of the larger primary schools in York and North Yorkshire Local Authorities agreed to participate in the study.

From these schools, every child in the first class of formal school (Reception class in England) was seen individually to assess their expressive vocabulary as measured by a picture naming test (Wechsler, 2004); we also included in the screening simple tests of letter knowledge, reading and writing. Children with known sensory impairments, behavioural difficulties, poor attendance, and those with English as an additional language (EAL) were excluded from further participation, as were children in three schools in which children performed at a high level.

Next, children from the 20 remaining schools were ranked, within schools, in order of their vocabulary scores (adjusted for age), and the 10 children with the lowest Picture Naming scores were selected as possible candidates for intervention. Each of these children was seen again to undergo an individual assessment. During this session we assessed verbal skills in two ways: testing vocabulary (here, the ability to provide definitions of words and verbal reasoning skills (e.g., you wear these to keep your hands warm ... what are they?). We also assessed non-verbal ability. We then selected the 8 children per class who performed most poorly on the verbal tests to receive the intervention. One school then withdrew, leaving a total of 152 children in 19 schools (75 boys and 77 girls).

Ethical approval for this study was given by the University of York, Department of Psychology Ethics Committee. Consent for the screening phase was provided by the head teachers of participating schools and by parents and carers for all children who received individual assessment or intervention.

THE RESEARCH PROTOCOL

The method we chose to evaluate the effects of the intervention was a randomized controlled trial. We saw in Chapter 2 that this method is the 'gold standard' for intervention trials.

With parental permission, 152 children were allocated at random to receive either the P + R Intervention or the OL Intervention. As is to be expected, given random allocation, the two groups did not differ in terms of gender, number of children receiving free school meals, behaviour problems or attendance. An overview of the study, including details of the selection and allocation of the participants, is provided in Figure 4.1.

We describe the content and delivery of the interventions in the next two chapters. Here suffice it to say that both programmes were highly structured and used multi-sensory teaching techniques. Each lasted 20 weeks and was delivered by a teaching assistant whom we trained and supported. The P + R programme contained activities to promote **phoneme** awareness, letter-sound knowledge, **sight word** recognition, simple writing and awareness of print and reading strategies. The OL programme in contrast contained activities to promote listening and speaking skills and specifically targeted vocabulary and **narrative** skills, question generation and making **inferences**.

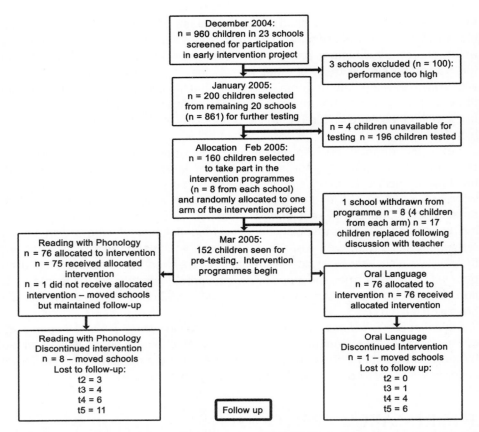

Figure 4.1 Overview of the intervention: the CONSORT diagram (Moher, Schulz and Altman, 2001)

MONITORING PROGRESS

The research team assessed the progress of the children in reading and language from pre-test (time 1, *t1*) through mid-test after 10 weeks (*t2*), post-test at the end of the 20-week intervention (*t3*) and six months after the intervention had ceased to assess maintenance of gains (*t4*). We also followed up the children a year later at time *t5* towards the end of the first phase of schooling (Key Stage 1 in England).

At each assessment point, we had a long test protocol. Given the nature of the trial it was important to assess gains in reading-related and language-related skills in *both* groups of children. Rather than focusing on the precise tests we used (you can read about them in our journal article: Bowyer-Crane et al., 2008), we will describe the skills we measured. It is important to note that, in practice, such comprehensive assessment would not be needed – or indeed be practicable – for monitoring the progress of children in an intervention.

Key measures in our battery were tests of **phoneme** awareness, early literacy measures (the ability to read words that are highly frequent in young children's books, and the ability to write one's own name) and tests of vocabulary and grammatical skills. We included a test of letter knowledge and three tests of **phoneme** awareness. The first was a **phoneme** detection task in which children were asked to repeat three-**phoneme** nonwords (e.g., *bip*), and then to state the sound which was either in the first or last position (e.g., *b* or *p*). In the second, the child heard all but the last **phoneme** of a single syllable word shown in a picture and was required to complete the word by providing the final **phoneme** (e.g., *boa ? [t]*). Lastly we assessed **phoneme** blending (putting **phonemes** together to make words), **phoneme** segmentation (breaking words down into separate **phonemes**) and **phoneme** deletion (taking **phonemes** out of words to make a new word). To assess skills more directly related to literacy, we used tests of single word reading, letter-sound knowledge, letter writing, spelling and nonword reading.

Our assessment of oral language skills included a test of **narrative** in which children were told a story illustrated by pictures and then had to re-tell it using the pictures as prompts. **Narratives** were recorded and later transcribed to provide two measures: how much of the initial story's content was recalled and the average length of the sentences used. We also measured children's knowledge of words that were taught in the OL intervention and their expressive **grammar** using a set of picture cards with corresponding questions, designed to elicit a variety of grammatical structures (e.g., talking about events using the past tense). Finally, we assessed listening and reading comprehension using parallel tasks.

THE FINDINGS

To analyse our data, we focused on the outcomes for the children at *t3* (at the end of the intervention) and at *t4* (six months after the intervention finished). Full details of the data and statistical analyses are given in our paper (Bowyer-Crane et al., 2008); these took account of the fact that there were two groups of four children in 19 different schools. Often when researchers evaluate the efficacy of a treatment, they compare people given the treatment with people who either get the same treatment later (waiting control) or who get an alternative treatment which isn't expected to affect the skills that the main treatment is trying to improve (a 'placebo' treatment). Here the approach was rather different because we were comparing the effects of two alternative treatments (P + R or OL); everyone got some extra attention which probably in and of itself was beneficial. Thus, we looked for differential benefits of the two intervention programmes and tested our predictions that:

1   Children who received the P + R programme would do better on tests of **phoneme** awareness, letter-sound knowledge, basic reading and spelling skills than children who received the OL programme.
2   Children who received the OL programme would do better on tests of vocabulary, **grammar**, **narrative** and listening skills than children who received the P + L programme.
3   Progress would be sustained after the end of the intervention.

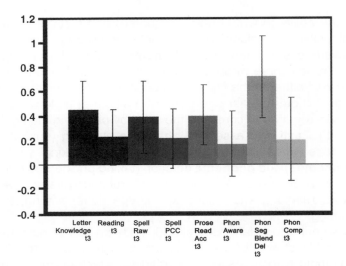

Figure 4.2 The relative benefits on reading-related tasks of children who received the P + R programme

It was encouraging to find that the results of our study were in line with our theoretical expectations. After we had taken the necessary step of controlling for entry level skills, there were differences in the attainments of the children who received the different programmes. Figure 4.2 shows the relative benefits to the children who received the P + R programme (compared with their peers who received OL intervention) on test of reading and phonological skills at the end of the intervention. The gains they made in letter knowledge, spelling, prose reading accuracy and segmenting and blending were significantly greater than those made by the children in the OL group, confirming that the P + R training was effective. These relative gains were maintained six months latter when they also did better on a test of non-word reading, suggesting that the teaching had promoted independent phonic decoding skills.

We now turn to the relative benefits to the children who received the OL programme (compared with their peers who received the P + R intervention). Here our findings complemented those described above. As shown in Figure 4.3, the gains made at the end of the intervention in vocabulary and **grammar** were significantly greater than the gains made by the P + R group, and gains in **narrative** skills were marginally so. However, disappointingly, these children were not much ahead of their peers in listening comprehension or in reading comprehension skills.

Another way of considering these findings is in terms of how well these intervention programmes could 'lift' children from the 'at-risk' to the typical range of reading and language skills for their age. We were able to examine this issue because we had available data from some 500 of these children's classroom peers at time *t4* of the study. Figure 4.4 shows the relative standing of the children who received the intervention compared to their classmates on tests of letter-knowledge, reading, spelling, vocabulary and **grammar** skills. The findings

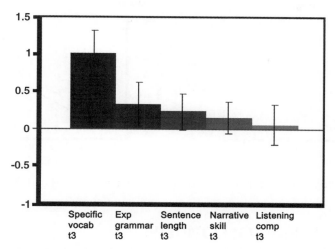

Figure 4.3 The relative benefits on language-related tasks of children who received the OL programme

are important. After just 20 weeks of targeted intervention, the recipient of these programmes were mostly performing within the average range on literacy skills for those who received the P + R programme, and on oral language skills for those who received the OL programme.

With respect to reading development, a **standard score** below 85 was used to classify children as being 'at-risk' of literacy difficulties. At the end of the intervention, 68.1% of the OL group remained at-risk on this criterion compared with only 50% of the P + R group. Moreover, 7.1% of children in the P + R group now had above average reading scores (greater than 115), while none of the OL children had scores in this range.

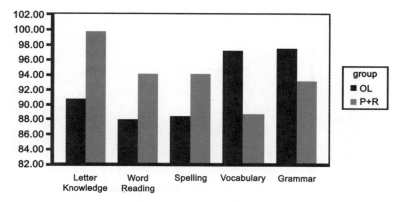

Figure 4.4 Performance of children from the OL and P + R groups on tests of letter knowledge, reading, spelling, vocabulary and grammar skills – expressed in terms of standard scores relative to classroom peers.

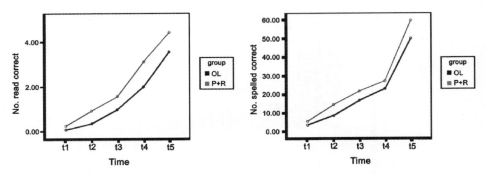

Figure 4.5   Progress in reading and spelling over time in the P + R and OL groups

LONGER TERM FOLLOW-UP

When the children who had received the intervention were about 7 years old, we re-assessed their word reading, spelling and **grammar** skills on the same tests we had used before. This was some 15 months after the intervention ended. In Figure 4.5, it can be seen that the two groups had continued to make progress in reading and spelling skills. Similarly, Figure 4.6 shows that they continued to make gains in their performance on the **grammar** test. However by *t5*, the only measure on which the groups differed statistically was **grammar**, where the advantage for the OL group was maintained.

Unfortunately, here we are confronted with a limitation in our research method. Because the trial did not include an untreated control group, we have no way of knowing what the longer term benefits of the interventions were in absolute terms. This is because we do not know what progress might have been seen over the same time course in the absence of any intervention. Moreover, in these follow-up

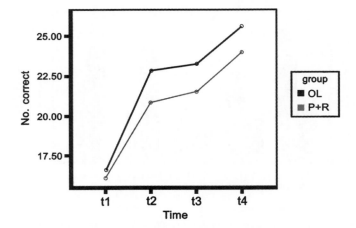

Figure 4.6   Progress in grammar over time in the P + R and OL groups

data, we have something referred to as a null result; children in the two groups –
who had received either the P + R and the OL intervention – no longer differed.
Such null results are impossible to interpret definitively. It is worth noting, however,
what the possible interpretations are. First, and most disappointing, would be that
the positive effects of the P + R intervention for reading had washed out after 15
months. Second, and the interpretation we favour for obvious reasons, is that both
interventions had a positive effect on reading in the longer term. Indeed we think
there is every reason to suppose that children whose oral language skills are
boosted will be better able to respond to the literacy curriculum than children with
oral language difficulties, and hence they may have been able to get off to a much
better start as a result of intervention than they would otherwise have done. But
to clinch this issue of course requires further research!

CONCLUSIONS

We have argued that to be well-founded, educational interventions should be
theoretically motivated and evidence-based. Our starting point was with the theory
that both proficient decoding and competent language comprehension are required in order to read for meaning. From this theory, we developed two intervention programmes: one targeting basic reading and phonological skills and one
targeting oral language abilities. We designed these programmes to be suitable for
children in the first year in school who have poorly developed speech and language
skills, to be delivered by trained teaching assistants. After 20 weeks of intervention,
we found that both intervention programmes were effective in promoting basic
skills that underlie reading comprehension: the P + R programme led to improvements in reading accuracy, spelling and **phoneme** awareness while the OL
programme fostered vocabulary and grammatical skills.

Our findings show conclusively that early intervention programmes can be
delivered successfully by teaching assistants to 5- and 6-year- olds at risk of
literacy difficulties. It is because we want to tell people about how worthwhile these
approaches are that we decided to write this book. The programmes which we
describe are suitable for children in the very early stages of reading instruction.

Chapter 5

The Phonology with Reading Programme

The programme draws on two widely used programmes, *Sound Linkage* and *Jolly Phonics*. In developing the **Phonology** with Reading (P + R) programme we were also guided by The National Reading Panel's recommendations for effective early literacy interventions which drew on evidence-based practice (National Reading Panel, 2000).

As we have seen, learning to read depends upon two basic foundation skills: knowing the sounds of letters, and **phoneme** awareness – the ability to work with the sounds in words. Having these skills gives children a 'self-teaching' strategy – a way to work out unknown words on their own, without always having to rely on a teacher or parent. In addition, the sounding out process can be an important memory tool – each time a word is sounded out successfully, the link between the sounds and letters is made stronger and the child gets closer to knowing that word 'by sight'.

In English, however, there are many irregular words meaning that the sounding out process is not always straightforward. Nonetheless, teaching the sounds of letters in combination with **phoneme** awareness provides an excellent helpful way to help children develop their reading skills. For this reason, letter learning and working with sounds take up a major part of each intervention session. Using these skills in combination is typically referred to as *phonics*.

Many other programmes have been developed to help children to learn to read. We wanted to base our programme on what had worked well in the past.

Sound Linkage is the reading intervention programme we discussed in Chapter 2. It is aimed at struggling readers of around 6 to 10 years of age. This programme in turn builds on some of the ideas of Reading Recovery (Clay, 1985)

Developing Language and Literacy: Effective Intervention in the Early Years
By Julia M. Carroll, Claudine Bowyer-Crane, Fiona J. Duff, Charles Hulme, and Margaret J. Snowling
© 2011 John Wiley & Sons, Ltd

but also includes structured **phonics** work. The programme has four key parts: reading and re-reading books; letter learning, training in phonological awareness and writing a story. Each session is individual and planned around a child's strengths and weaknesses. Children are encouraged to read books more than once, to help increase their confidence, build their 'sight vocabulary' and develop their skills. Each session has a few key learning points which are emphasised in different ways. Many different strategies can be used to emphasise the same learning point; for example, children are encouraged to write a newly learnt letter in many different contexts (in the air, on paper, in sand and so on) and will be asked to write words involving that letter. Teaching assistants are encouraged to select from a range of possible activities to support that child's abilities. The programme also emphasises the link between phonological awareness and written language (that's why it is called *Sound Linkage*).

As we have seen, this programme is effective. However, it is aimed at older children who have already fallen behind their peers in reading. We knew that we would have to make some changes to the programme to make it suitable for younger, beginning readers, so we looked for other research ideas to incorporate.

A meta-analysis of reading research was recently carried out in America. A meta-analysis is a study which brings together most of the key research on a topic to make some general conclusions on what works well. Part of the meta-analysis focused on phonics teaching and drew some interesting conclusions.

The review found the following to be particularly useful:

1. **phonics** programmes that focus on a few key phonological skills (normally segmenting and blending sounds) rather than a wide mixture of skills (such as finding rhyming words, matching sounds across words, or swapping sounds in different words);
2. programmes that include small group work rather than whole class or individual programmes;
3. programmes that work with younger readers (those considered to be 'at-risk') rather than those implemented after children had failed; and
4. relatively short-term interventions with a focus on **phonics** (with a total intervention time of between 5 and 18 hours).

We therefore decided to incorporate these ideas into our **phonics** intervention. We would focus on segmenting and blending, the key skills for sounding out words, and we would use a combination of small group and individual tuition.

One of the most widely used programme for teaching letters and sounds in the UK at the time of writing is *Jolly Phonics* (http://www.jollylearning.co.uk). This is a programme in which children are taught actions to help them link sounds with letters.

For example, when the children are taught the letter 'r', they hear a story about a puppy who likes to rip up rags. The puppy makes a growling 'rrrr' sound while ripping up rags, and the children learn to make this sound and pretend to be a puppy when they see the letter 'r'. The page introducing the 'rr' sound is shown in Figure 5.1. As you can imagine, children love this system! It is fun, but it also

R r

ACTION

Pretend to be a puppy pulling a rag, with teeth clenched and shaking bead, saying *rrrr.*

rag
run
rabbit
forest
carrot

Draw the letters dotted here:

Figure 5.1 Worksheet for introducing the 'r' sound, from the Phonics Handbook (by kind permission of Jolly Learning Limited)

makes good sense from a learning perspective. Children are using all of their senses when learning. Not only do they see the letter and hear the sound, they make the sound and an action as well. This is multi-sensory learning and it helps in all kinds of learning situations.

Jolly Phonics was created as a programme to use with a whole class. Teachers are encouraged to introduce a new letter every day, and to help the children begin segmenting and blending words as soon as they have a few letters to help them. The emphasis on letter learning, segmenting and blending was just what we were looking for. The fact that lots of schools already use this programme was another bonus. However, since we were working with the weaker children in the class, we felt it would be useful to make a few changes to how the programme was introduced. We suggested introducing a letter every second day, and spending plenty of time on revision every time a group of six letters has been learnt. We also used a highly structured way of teaching segmenting and blending. Weaker readers often have difficulties with understanding how to segment and blend sounds to make words, and so we wanted to teach this in a very gradual and thorough way.

We included two types of book reading in the programme (see Appendix 5.1). Children are expected to be reading short books from the start of training, rather than waiting until most of the letter sounds have been introduced. This is because many of these children will already have been introduced to the letter sounds and it is important now to develop all of the relevant literacy skills.

Regular book-work allows children to link basic phonic skills with reading in context. However, weak reading skills may hold children back from reading books that they find fun – early reading books have very simple (sometimes boring!) stories. For this reason the book work is divided into two types:

1. Group book work provides an opportunity to introduce children to stimulating picture books. It is also used to provide a link to the letter and sound work of that day.
2. Individual book work provides the opportunity for children to practise their reading skills with books at the right level for them as individual learners.

See Appendix 5.1 for examples of book titles.

Finally, we included some activities intended to boost **sight word** knowledge in the intervention. While learning letters and sounding out skills are crucial for growth in literacy, sounding out alone will not be a successful strategy in English, because English has some words that are irregular – that is, sounding them out letter by letter would not lead to the correct spoken word. In fact, Janet Vousden at the University of Warwick (Vousden, 2008) found that sounding out every word would only allow you to read around 60% of English text correctly. This turns out to be because some of the most common words in the language (such as 'I', 'she', 'of', 'come', and 'was') are irregular. It therefore makes sense to teach common irregular words in addition to letter-sound correspondences because this substantially increases the amount of text that can be read.

The programme was developed for use with children towards the end of their first year of formal schooling (reception year in English schools). At this stage, the teacher would normally have introduced all of the letter sounds to the class, and would have covered segmenting and blending of simple words. Most of the class would therefore be ready to begin reading books and working out words themselves. The programme is aimed at children who have had that class teaching, but for some reason have not been able to use it to develop their sounding out skills. We aim to reinforce the letter learning and **phonics** skills, while also trying to develop reading strategies. The reading with **phonology** intervention therefore has four key activities:

1. letter learning
2. **phoneme** awareness (segmenting and blending)
3. book reading
4. **sight word** learning.

How and why we cover each of these skills is summarised in Table 5.1.

GENERAL TEACHING PRINCIPLES

Before we proceed, a quick reminder of the key aspects of good teaching practice that are important to bear in mind when implementing this intervention programme:

Table 5.1 Summary of the intervention activities

Key Skills	Why?	How?
Letter learning	To develop self-teaching abilities	Using the *Jolly Phonics* framework
Phoneme awareness	To develop self-teaching abilities	Using gradual **scaffolding** techniques
Group book reading	To develop enjoyment of books and link phonological awareness with reading	Using a 'real' story book in the group session
Individual book reading	To develop individual reading skills	Using repeated practice with books at the easy and instructional levels
Sight word learning	To allow children to read key irregular words	Using repeated practice and multi-sensory learning

1. *Little and often (the theory of distributed practice):* Children learn best if they are taught little and often, if they revise what they have learnt regularly, and if they use their knowledge in different contexts.
2. *Use all your senses (teach using a multisensory approach):* Children with learning difficulties learn most effectively when they bring all their senses to bear – teach new concepts through sight, hearing, speaking, and feeling.
3. *Avoid learning confusion:* Children learn best if they are taught one thing at a time – one letter, one word, or one skill. Two items learnt at the same time are more likely to be confused later.
4. *'Shape' complex behaviour:* To teach children a complex skill, move in small sequential steps from simple to complex. Model the behaviour yourself, and provide prompts to encourage the behaviour. Praise the child for gradual approximations towards a learning goal. This is known as '**scaffolding**'. **Scaffolding** means that within a group you can ask individual children to work at the level that they can manage, always trying to move them on to the next level gradually and with support.
5. *Encourage 'deep' learning:* Children learn best when they are encouraged to work out rules for themselves and when they are helped to correct their own errors. Give examples and encourage children to derive the rule for themselves.

STRUCTURE OF THE PROGRAMME

The P + R Programme is taught over a period of 20 weeks in daily sessions. The first week is spent introducing the children to the routine and to the materials, and assessing the level that they are starting at. There are then alternating group and individual sessions in blocks of three weeks. Time is included in the programme to allow plenty of consolidation. The group sessions provide a chance for children to

Table 5.2 Structure of individual and group sessions

Group (30 minutes)	Individual (20 minutes)
Ice Breaker - story/poem - revision of letter 4 minutes	*Revision* revise/reinforce sound(s) learned so far 2 minutes
Sound of the Day (Jolly Phonics) - story - action - writing letter 8 minutes	*Phonological Awareness* - segmentation *OR* blending exercises 3 minutes **Sight word** work - work on **sight word** vocabulary 5 minutes
Book Work - book for the sound of the day, - teacher led 'shared' reading 8 minutes *Phonological awareness* - segmentation *OR* blending exercises 5 minutes *Plenary* - sound of the day - sticker - smiley/sad face 5 minutes	*Reading books* - reading an **easy book** - re-reading a book at **instructional level** - reading a new book 10 minutes

enjoy books as a group and to learn from each other, while the individual sessions provide a chance to focus on each individual child's weaknesses. After each session we asked the teaching assistants to record what the children had done and learnt, so that they had a record of their progress and any weaknesses.

Both the group and individual teaching sessions of the programme follow a clear structure. This structure is outlined in the Table 5.2. The timings are flexible, but we did ask that teaching assistants cover each part of the programme.

THE INDIVIDUAL ACTIVITIES

Icebreaker

Each session began with an 'ice-breaker' in which the children practised naming the letters they had seen in the past, and settled into the session. Normally, this would simply involve the teaching assistant running through a set of flash cards with the previously learnt letters on them, and asking the children to give the sounds and actions for each letter. Of course, this set got longer every time the children learnt a new letter.

Sound of the Day

In each group session, a different letter was introduced in the manner described in the *Jolly Phonics* handbook. A short story is told about the action that links to the letter. For example, for the letter 'f', the children were told a story about squashing the air out of an inflatable fish, and how this makes the sound of air escaping at the same time ('fffff'). Children then pretend to squash out the air and make the sound and action. Once they have got the sound and action, children practice writing the letter in the air, on white boards and finally in their workbooks.

Most of the time, the children in our intervention had already been introduced to the letter in classroom teaching. However, in many cases the knowledge of the letter was not secure — typically they may fail to recognise it in different contexts or they might recognise it on some days but not others. For effective sounding out, letter sounds need to be automatic. If a child is struggling to remember a letter, they will find it hard to remember the other things needed for long enough to sound out a word successfully! For that reason we felt it was important that children had plenty of practice with letters and became automatic in giving letter sounds.

Group Book Work

For each group session we selected a short, fun, story book that included words with the target sound of the day. For example, on the day the letter 't' was introduced, the book was *The Tiger Who Came to Tea*. This part of the programme meant that children experienced and learnt about interesting books, and it made clear the links between reading, sounds and letters for the children, because the phonological awareness exercises followed directly from words in the stories.

We used guidelines for the group book reading to ensure that all of the group were actively involved in the work and were following the story. In classroom situations, it is often the children with the weakest reading related skills who find it hard to focus on story books and understand the story. We wanted to make sure that all of the children understood how books work (where the writing is and what it means, for example) as well as what was going on in the story.

Therefore we asked the teaching assistant to finger point to words as she read them. We also chose books that had key repeated phrases (such as 'fee fie fo fum' in *Jack and the Beanstalk*) and we encouraged the children to say the phrases along with the teaching assistant while reading. After they had finished the story, the group took a minute or two to discuss the story and what had happened. In these ways, children are actively involved and the teaching assistant can check their understanding afterwards.

The group story reading leads directly on to the phonological awareness tasks. We produced a table which listed an optional song to introduce the letter, the group reading book to be used, and some examples of words of different lengths that could be used for the segmenting and blending tasks. An example for the first three group sessions is shown in Table 5.3.

Table 5.3 Summary of activities and example words for each day

Letter Group 1	Poem/Song of the day	Book	Segmenting and Blending Activities			
			Multi syllable	CV or VC	CVC	Clusters
S	Snake is slowly slithering over the soft, soft ground. 'ssss' Is his soft little hissing sound. *tune: nobody likes me	*Sam Sheep can't sleep*	See-saw sandwich Sausage Strawberry Squirrel	Sea, saw, us	Sun, Sam, sad, sat, sock Horse, bus, kiss	Snake, sleep grass
A	When all of the ants are on the ground I do not make a single sound But when the ants crawl on my arm I say 'a, a, a' 'til they all crawl away. tune: this old man	*Cat on the mat*	Apple, ambulance Arrow Angelina Aeroplane	at, add	Sack, cat, man, bat	Ant, pant, flag
T	t, t, t, t is the sound of the tennis ball. t, t, t, t Over the net so tall tune: row row row your boat.	*The tiger who came to tea*	tomato, tiger, tennis, telephone, Teletubbies	toe, tea, tie, at	Ten, tap, toes Sat, coat, pot, night	Tent, spot Mist, skirt, paint

Phonological Awareness: Segmenting and Blending Activities

There has been a great deal of research investigating the links between phonological awareness and learning to read. We now know that children are able to work with syllables before they are able to work with smaller sounds such as **phonemes**. We also know that **phoneme** awareness is the type of phonological awareness that is most important for learning to read and spell. In particular, segmenting and blending tasks, where a child breaks up a word into its sounds or combines a list of sounds into a word, link closely to the tasks of reading and spelling, respectively. This is why we chose to concentrate on these skills.

The teaching assistant selects some words from that day's book to use for segmenting and blending exercises. For example, a child who is still working on syllables could be asked to break up 'tiger' into two parts, and a child who is starting to be able to work with **phonemes** could be asked to break up 'tea' into two sounds. A more advanced child should be able to work with a longer word such as 'stripe'. We know that it is harder for children to segment words containing consonant blends (two or more consonants together, such as the 'str' at the start of 'stripe'). Therefore children should only be asked to do this after they are secure in segmenting and blending simpler words.

We also encouraged the teaching assistants to work with words with the target sound at different points of the word, so that children experienced the sound in different contexts. For example, one child might be asked to segment the sounds in 'tap', a second the sounds in 'pet' and another to segment 'water', with the 't' sound in the middle rather than at the beginning or end.

It is not always easy to know how many **phonemes** there are in a word! **Phonemes** usually, but not always, correspond to single letters. There are some letters which correspond to more than one **phoneme**, and some **phonemes** that correspond to more than one letter (see Appendix 8.2)

Children often find segmenting and blending quite difficult, and there is a good deal of variation in how quickly individual children grasp the concepts. For this reason we use a '**scaffolding**' approach. Scaffolding means that within a group you can ask individual children to work at the level that they can manage, always trying to move them on to the next level gradually and with support (or '**scaffolding**').

The level of difficulty of the task is determined by the length of the word used and by what the child is asked to do. We talk about 'stretching' sounds as an intermediate level between a word and a set of separate **phonemes**. At first, children are asked to 'stretch out' the word, before being asked to separate the **phonemes**. They start with two **phoneme** words (such as 'at' or 'tea') and go on to longer words, and finally words with consonant blends and more than one syllable. This is shown in Box 5.1.

- Stage 1: Stretch the word
- Stage 2: Teaching assistant illustrates how many sounds there are with counters and repeats the stretched word.

Tutor:	'Can you stretch this word for me: bat?'
Child:	'bbbbbaaaaattttt'
T:	'Good. Now, this word has 3 sounds [put three counters in front of the child]. What is the first sound you hear?'
Ch:	'bbbbbb'
T:	'Good.' [push one counter forward] 'Bbb-aattt. What's the next sound?'
Ch:	'aaaa'
T:	'Good.' [push next counter forward] 'Bb-aa, bbbaaatttt. What's the sound at the end?'
Ch:	'tttt'
T:	'Good, now say all the sounds.'
Ch:	'Bb-aa-ttt. [tutor pushes the corresponding counter as the child says the sound].

Box 5.1   Segmenting the word bat in a gradual way

- Stage 3: Teaching assistant repeats the stretched word and lets the child push counters forwards.
- Stage 4: Teaching assistant repeats the word normally.

Producing Sounds

Some children had trouble actually producing the target sounds for some of the letters. In our intervention, we gave these children some exercises developed by a speech therapist to work on using their mouth and tongue correctly to make sounds.

For example, if a child found the 'th' sounds difficult to make, they could be encouraged to bring their tongue to their lips to make the sound, first by licking their lips, and by trying out different exercises to help them become more aware of what their tongue was doing while making the sound.

Sometimes, if a child does have difficulties in producing sounds, this can lead them to have difficulties recognising the sound in different words (for example, knowing whether 'think' should be spelled as 'think' or 'fink'). It was for this reason that we felt it was important to emphasise the difference in pronunciation between some sounds for some children.

Activities to Promote 'Sight Word' Reading

Five minutes in the individual sessions is spent on learning a new word 'by sight'. The teaching assistant keeps a list of the words a child knows, and introduces a new one in each individual session. The child practices writing the word on different surfaces (such as a whiteboard and in sand), saying it, making it with magnetic letters and so on. They could also recognise it in different places (for example, in a book or on a wall-chart).

As with letter learning, it is important that children use as many senses as possible when trying to learn new words. That is why we encouraged teaching assistants to use a wide range of different learning situations.

Individual Book Work

At the end of each individual session, the child is asked to read two books, or, if they are very much a beginner, sentences written by the teaching assistant.

First, they re-read a book that had been introduced before, then they read a new book for the first time. We ask that the teaching assistant keeps a '**running record**' while the child re-reads the book, so that they know how accurate the child is. We aim for the children to be reading books with 95% accuracy (meaning that they make a mistake with only 1 out of 20 words) before they move on to a harder book. If they came to a word they do not know, they are helped to sound out or to try and work out the word from context.

The books we used were graded in a very careful way, as recommended by Peter Hatcher (Hatcher, 2000b). This grading system takes account of how many words there are in the book, how many longer words there are, how long the sentences used are, and how complex the **grammar** in the book is. It provides a sensitive measure of how complex the book will be to read, which is standardised across many different reading schemes. A list of books graded using this system is available at: http://www.cumbria.gov.uk/childrensservices/reading/books/viewlist.asp.

This practice and repetition with books means that children encounter the same words on a few occasions, giving them more time to learn these words. It also helps them gain confidence and to read with understanding. On the first read through of a book, a child will be working out many words. On a second read through, they can concentrate more on the meanings of the words and so understand the story more.

Plenary

At the end of each session, five minutes are allocated for a plenary session. This is a chance to ensure that children have learnt the sound and letter of the day. The children are asked to say the sound they have learnt and to practice drawing the letter of the day in the air. Often, they draw that letter on a plain sticker, which they then put on their sweater for the rest of the day.

Plenary time is another opportunity to consolidate what the children have learnt and to encourage them to reflect on their learning. Children at this stage are only just beginning to become aware of their own learning processes. Until a child understands what they find easy or hard, or starts to think about what they have learnt, they don't understand the role of practice or rehearsal in learning. Older children can practice things they need to learn (such as spellings, or lines in a play), but younger children aren't necessarily aware that practice can be helpful. The plenary time encourages them to start to think about their own learning.

Consolidation

Two days of consolidation work were planned once the children had been taught a set of 6 letters and sounds. This was time to go over the letters and words that have been learnt in a variety of different ways, including versions of games such as snap, twister and I-spy, and some writing work. Again, practicing what children have learnt in a new context will help to ensure that their knowledge is well established.

SUMMARY

Overall, the P + R programme aimed to provide a strong foundation for early literacy development for children with weak language skills in their first year of school. It focused on a few key skills: letter learning, book reading, segmenting, blending and **sight word** learning. These skills have all been shown to be crucial for early word reading. If all the skills are well developed, the child is well placed to begin reading relatively independently and working out words for him or herself.

Throughout the programme, we aimed to use five general learning principles which are based on research as well as good teaching practice. These are: teaching little and often; use all of the senses; avoiding learning confusion; shaping complex skills; and encouraging 'deep' learning.

Chapter 6

The Oral Language Programme

We saw in Chapter 1 that 'oral language' is a key component in the development of reading, and in particular of reading comprehension. Oral language is a multidimensional construct made up of a number of different skills that contribute to a child's communication (***expressive language***), and understanding (***receptive language***). Skills such as vocabulary knowledge, awareness of **grammar** and **syntax**, and knowledge of **narrative** structure, are all fundamental to the development of successful reading comprehension. In addition, these skills are vital for developing a child's written language and enabling them to access a curriculum with ever increasing demands. Thus, oral language does not just underlie successful literacy development, but is one of the key building blocks for success during the school years and beyond.

The Oral Language (OL) Programme targets several areas of oral language. We developed the programme for beginning readers, with the aim of improving their **receptive** and **expressive language** skills in the hope that this would help foster their emerging literacy skills. The programme is designed to help improve children's listening, speaking and **inferencing** skills, as well as increasing their vocabulary and knowledge of story structure.

The programme has been written to encourage active participation on the part of the child. Children are taught using multisensory techniques within a repetitive framework. The activities have been designed to be enjoyable and to encourage the children to engage with their peers and the teacher. The teacher is assisted in each session by 'Sam the Bear'; a teddy bear who is introduced in the first session and around whom many of our activities have been created. However, Sam's main function is to choose the recipient of the Best Listener Award at the end of each group session (see below). The techniques used in this programme are based on what is recognised as best practice for oral language interventions. In addition, the vocabulary training adopted is based on the multiple-context

Developing Language and Literacy: Effective Intervention in the Early Years
By Julia M. Carroll, Claudine Bowyer-Crane, Fiona J. Duff, Charles Hulme, and Margaret J. Snowling
© 2011 John Wiley & Sons, Ltd

approach proposed by Isobel Beck and colleagues at the University of Pittsburgh (Beck, McKeown and Kucan, 2002). Vocabulary instruction included nouns, verbs, comparatives and question words, selected as age-appropriate, instructional and relevant to the topics covered in the teaching blocks. The programme also incorporates the objectives for oral language development proposed in the UK National Literacy Strategy of England at the time of writing (DfES, 2001). By drawing together ideas from diverse sources we have produced a comprehensive intervention programme covering a number of different skills underlying oral language development. The remainder of this chapter consists of a detailed guide to the structure and activities used in the original programme. A session by session guideline from the original programme is available from the authors detailing the vocabulary and activities covered in each session. However, the structure, techniques and activities incorporated in the programme can be adapted to teach whatever vocabulary and language skills are appropriate for the children you are working with.

PROGRAMME STRUCTURE

The Language Intervention Programme is designed to run over a 20 week period, further divided into two 10 week modules. Each 10-week module starts with an initial introduction week, the purpose of which is to introduce the children to the programme and materials, to familiarise them with the structure of the sessions and to establish a group identity. During this week, children are also assessed to provide a baseline against which to monitor children's progress over the course of the intervention. This assessment is then repeated in the final week of each 10-week module.

The remaining 9 weeks of each module are divided into three-week topic blocks, each concentrating on a specific topic area. We selected topic areas in consultation with teachers and practitioners to reflect areas of the curriculum that children would typically be studying at this age. These were 'ourselves', 'things we wear', 'my family', 'growing', 'journeys' and 'time'. Children received two weeks of explicit instruction, consisting of sessions targeting new vocabulary and developing key language skills. This targeted block of sessions was followed by one week of consolidation activities in which they could revise vocabulary, as well as expand on the ideas and concepts taught in the preceding instruction weeks. For example, if they had learnt the verb 'to grow' in a teaching session, the teacher might introduce them to the past tense 'grew' or the present tense 'growing'.

As discussed in chapter 3, it is vital that children's progress is monitored over the course of the intervention. Planning and record sheets completed for each session provide an ongoing record of children's progress across the programme as a whole, while the **narrative** task provides an indication of children's progress in specific areas, notably use of **grammar** and story structure. When completing the **narrative** record, children produce a story to accompany a series of pictures. Initially the story is produced without support from the teacher. This therefore, provides an indication of the child's language ability and can be used to monitor a child's use of grammatical structures, use of connectives (ways of combining two sentences, e.g., and, because), and use of vocabulary. Finally, children are formally assessed in the final week of each 10-week module.

SESSION STRUCTURE

The programme incorporates a mixture of group and individual sessions, alternating on a daily basis. The individual sessions allow teachers to tailor the intervention to the needs of each individual child, while the group sessions are aimed at improving children's **expressive language** skills by giving children the opportunity to share ideas and ask questions in a safe environment. *Group sessions* are designed to last approximately 30 minutes and to incorporate a number of key activities. The left column of Table 6.1 shows the structure for each

Table 6.1 Structure of sessions in instruction weeks

Group session	Individual Session
Introduction: Greet the children, and get them settled into the session. Introduce the day of the week, and talk about the best listener. (5 minutes)	Introduction: Greet the children and get them settled into the session. (2 minutes)
Multi-Sensory Learning: Teach new vocabulary using multi-sensory techniques. (5 minutes)	Vocabulary revision: Using the picture prompts and materials from the group sessions, revise the nouns, verbs and other vocabulary covered in the last group session. Particular attention should be paid to words the child found difficult to grasp. (5 minutes)
Reinforcement: Revise and reinforce vocabulary introduced in the last session. (7 minutes)	Narrative task: In this section of the session, the child is shown a three or four sequence picture story and asked to tell the story. A record is made of what the child says and the story is revisited in the next individual session. (5 minutes)
Speaking/Listening/Inferencing This section concentrates on targeting specific skills. (10 minutes)	Listening, Speaking and Inferencing This is an opportunity to target one or more skills that the child needs to work on. Examples of activities to be used can be found later in this chapter. (5 minutes)
Plenary The session is revisited in sequence. Sam chooses the best listener who puts their name on the best listener board. If time allows, a nursery rhyme is shared with the children (see Appendix 6.2). (3 minutes)	Plenary The session is brought to a close by going over with the child what they have done in the session and giving the child a sticker. (3 minutes)

group session in the core instruction weeks with suggested times for each section of the session. The introduction and consolidation weeks differ slightly in structure from the teaching weeks as the activities can be more varied. In short, the introduction and consolidation sessions should always begin and end in the same way as the core instruction sessions – with an introduction and a plenary. However, the remainder of the session can contain any relevant activities that the teacher feels would achieve her objectives. For example, an introduction session might include a game that encourages children to get to know each other, while for a consolidation session, the teacher might want to put together an activity that encourages children to use their new vocabulary in different contexts. Example session plans from the introduction, core instruction and consolidation weeks can be found in Appendix 6.1.

Individual sessions are designed to last for 20 minutes. The right hand column of Table 6.1 shows the structure of an individual session for use when planning these sessions. Activities should always be selected to be appropriate taking account of a child's own language level. For example, the teacher's initial assessment may indicate that a child can follow instructions containing one key word (i.e. pick up the *box*) but has difficulties with instructions containing two or more keywords (i.e. put the *box* on the *shelf*; put the *blue box* on the *shelf*; put the *blue box* on the *top shelf*). This then, is a skill that can be worked on in individual sessions by including activities that encourage the child to practice following instructions, starting at the two key-word level and gradually moving up to the four-word level as the child progresses. However, if the child would benefit more from practise with the structure of their oral communication, some alternative speaking activities could be used in the first few individual sessions. As the programme runs its course, observations of individual children in the group will help the teacher know which activities to use in her plans for individual sessions.

KEY COMPONENTS OF THE INTERVENTION

Every group and individual session contains at least one activity focusing on the development of effective listening, independent speaking and making **inferences**. There are some excellent teaching resources available commercially and we drew on ideas in several published programmes when developing the OL programme (see Appendix 6.3). You can do this as well. However, to give you an idea, we provide below examples of some of the activities used in our programme; it is by no means an exhaustive list. Some of the activities target specific skills while others target a combination of skills. The information in brackets indicates whether these activities can be used in group or individual sessions.

Listening Skills

Listening is a key skill in the development of language and therefore careful listening is stressed during the programme. In addition to carrying out activities that

Alison Schroeder introduced the Best Listener Award in her intervention programme '*Time to Talk*' and we have adapted it for use in this programme. The Best Listener Award is given at the end of each group session by Sam the Bear. Sam is a teddy bear who 'helps' the teacher to carry out the intervention programme. Sam attends every group and individual session and many of the activities have been devised with Sam as a central character. Sam is introduced to the children in the first session of the programme and the children are told that Sam has four listening rules, which they will practice in every session. Sam's key role is to 'choose' the 'Best Listener' at the end of every group session. This reward does not always have to be given to the child who has sat quietly in every session, but may be given to a child who has made a concerted effort to improve their listening skills. The child awarded the Best Listener Award has their name displayed on the board until the next session. However, while only one child receives the award in each group session, it is important when giving the award that all of the children are given positive feedback.

Box 6.1   Best Listener Award

depend on children attending well, an explicit reward scheme is built into the programme that provides positive feedback for children who show development in their listening skills. Details of this award scheme, taken from *Time to Talk* (Schroeder, 2001) can be found in Box 6.1.

Figure 6.1 shows a poster that was displayed to remind children of how to listen and attend. They played a variety of games and took part in activities to encourage their listening skills, as outlined below.

Listening Activities

- *Barrier Games (Group/Individual):* See Figure 6.2. Place a barrier between each child or between yourself and the child you are working with. Give each child an activity to complete by following your instructions, for example, colouring or drawing a picture, moving around a map etc. At the end of the activity, you can look at the final piece of work to see whether or not the children were able to follow your instructions and whether all of the children interpreted your instructions in the same way.
- *Key Word Stories (Group/Individual):* Choose a short story book with a repeated word and ask the child/children to listen for the word as you read the story. Give them an action to do when they hear the word, for example, stand up, touch their nose, put their hands in the air.
- *Copy Cat (Group/Individual):* Make up sentences, or read sentences from a book and ask the child to repeat them. The sentences can begin quite simply and then increase in complexity. For example, you might start with the sentence 'The cat sat on the mat' but progress to something like 'The fat, black cat sat on the red, fluffy mat drinking smooth, creamy milk' and so on. If possible, use sentences

Figure 6.1 Listening rules poster

Figure 6.2 The barrier game

which practice new vocabulary or practice using different verb tenses. If you are using this activity in a group session you could ask the children to whisper the sentence to each other in turn. The last child then repeats the sentence out loud – is it the same sentence that you started with?

Independent Speaking

Throughout the programme, children are encouraged to engage in independent speaking activities. These activities are designed to develop children's use of **expressive language**. The key principles of modelling and **scaffolding** are vital in these activities.

- *Talkabout (Group/Individual):* Choose a page from a book or another picture of your choice. Show the child the picture and talk about it together. Ask the child to describe something in the picture, tell you what is happening, what someone is doing etc.
- *Show and Tell (Group/Individual):* Ask the child to bring along their reading book, a piece of work or something from home that they would like to tell you/the group about. Initially you may need to support the child/children in doing this by asking questions and leading the discussion. As the child progresses, try to reduce the amount of support you give and encourage them to speak independently. As a group activity this will also encourage good listening skills and you could support members of the group in asking questions about the item they are being shown.
- *Magic Sack (Group/Individual):* See Figure 6.3. Fill a gift bag, pillow case, shoe box or similar with pictures or objects, for example, small toys. Ask the child/children to choose an object/picture from the magic sack and describe it to you/the group so you have to guess what it is. You could include a theme for this activity, for example, shapes, animals, food, to fit in with the topic you are working on. For example, if you were working on the words rough and smooth you could include different textured items in your bag, such as sandpaper, shiny paper, smooth pebbles, etc. As a group activity this also encourages good listening.

Inferencing/Sequencing

Many children with poor language may become passive listeners who seem inattentive or 'lost' in the classroom. In addition, they frequently have difficulty with sequencing activities, perhaps because they do not use inner speech. A range of activities can be used to encourage such children to engage more actively with the language they hear. Here we describe some of the activities we incorporated in the OL programme.

- *What Will Happen If?' (Group/Individual):* Give the children scenarios and ask them to think about what will happen if. . .? For example:
  1. you drop an egg on the ground?
  2. you stick a pin in a balloon?

Figure 6.3   The magic sack

3. you hold an ice cube in your hand?
4. you leave the tops off your felt tip pens?
5. you kick a football at a window?
Encourage the children to talk about the possible outcomes with each other. As a group activity, this will also encourage independent speaking, question formation and listening.

• *If... Then' (Group/Individual):* This activity encourages children to make predictions about what might happen. This is an important skill for comprehension.

Figure 6.4 Examples of a picture sequence

Read out the sentence stems to the children and ask them to finish the sentence. As a group activity, this game can encourage independent speaking, question formation and listening skills.

1. If you are feeling sick, then. . .
2. If you bang your head, then. . .
3. If you forget a cake is in the oven, then. . .
4. If your pet is ill, then. . .
5. If you are hungry, then. . .

- *Picture Sequencing (Group/Individual):* See Figure 6.4. Use short sequences of pictures to reinforce story sequencing. Place the picture sequences on the table and talk about them with the child or children. Then ask the child to put them together in the correct order. If the child/children need help with this task, put the cards in the correct order for them and then tell the story, pointing to the appropriate picture as you speak. When the child/children become proficient at this you could increase the number of pictures in the sequence.

Vocabulary Instruction

As we have seen, successful vocabulary learning is best achieved using a multi-contextual method in which children are encouraged to use the word in context rather than simply being given a definition of the word. Vocabulary instruction is only one part of our intervention programme and the time spent on word learning is therefore much less than in a dedicated vocabulary instruction programme. However, we have applied the basic principles of multiple-context learning as a vocabulary teaching strategy (Beck, McKeown and Kucan, 2002):

1. Children are given the opportunity to guess the word from context, be it a verbal clue, picture or action.
2. Correct guesses are reinforced or the correct word is supplied if necessary.
3. Each child is encouraged to say the word aloud in order to establish a phonological representation.
4. The teacher gives the children a formal definition of the word.
5. Each new word is revised in the following session, and the children are encouraged to use the word in context. For example, when learning the verb 'fold' each child made a paper aeroplane; an activity in which they had to actively fold paper. In this way, children are actively engaging with the word and developing a clear understanding of its meaning.

Narrative Task

A significant part of the intervention programme focused on improving children's **narrative** skills. Working on oral **narrative** skills helps children to sequence events, use a wide range of vocabulary, and form grammatically complex sentences. Good **narrative** skills in turn feed into the development of successful written **narrative**. Work on **narrative** is embedded in group as well as individual sessions. A popular method of working on group **narrative** is to use a washing line story. We used variations of this task regularly throughout the programme. To do this task you simply hang up a piece of string to represent a washing line using blutac or drawing pins. Alternatively, you could draw a washing line onto a large sheet of A3 paper to stick on the wall. You then ask the children to 'hang' the story elements onto the washing line to create your story. Your story elements can be pictures or words representing characters, locations, and events. There are a number of different ways of using this activity, an example of which is given in Box 6.2.

We thought it would be useful to show how the individual **narrative** task worked in practice. We therefore illustrate below how one of our teaching assistants encouraged a child's **narrative** skills over a series of sessions. As you will remember from Chapter 3, in the first session the teacher shows the child a short, simple sequence of pictures and the child produces a short story largely unaided. The story is recorded word for word by the teacher acting as scribe. As the child progresses with this task and their stories get longer, it is sometimes necessary

- Hang a piece of string up to represent a washing line e.g. either using drawing pins in a pinboard, or constructing a tabletop one with sticks and string etc. If you don't have a washing line you could draw one on a piece of card or A3 paper and use blutack to hang up your pictures. Put your story cards in piles on the table (who, where, when, what).
- Introduce the activity by saying 'We are going to make up a story using our story cards. First we have to decide **WHO** our story is about. Then we have to decide **WHERE** our story takes place. We have to decide **WHEN** our story takes place and we have to decide **WHAT** happens.'
- 'We have some pictures to help us. We have some **WHO** pictures, some **WHERE** pictures, some **WHEN** pictures and some **WHAT** pictures (point to the appropriate cards).'
- Pick a **WHO** picture up yourself first, and hang it on the washing line. Ask the children 'Who is our story about?' Make up a sentence e.g. 'One day, a policeman was walking down the street...'
- Pick up a **WHERE** picture and hang it on the washing line. Ask the children 'Where did the story take place?' Make up a sentence e.g. 'The policemen went to the greengrocers to buy some bananas...'
- Pick up a **WHEN** picture and hang it on the washing line. Ask the children 'When did the story take place? Make up a sentence e.g. It was teatime; it was morning; it was just after breakfast; it was the dead of night etc...'
- Pick up a **WHAT** picture, and hang it on the washing line. Ask the children 'What happens in our story?' Make up a sentence using their ideas e.g. 'The policeman ate his banana.'
- Then go through the story again pointing at the pictures as you tell the story.
- You can extend this activity by adding **more pictures** i.e. pick more than one WHO card, more than one WHAT card etc.
- You can ask the children to pick the cards themselves.
- You could ask the children to predict **what happens next**, and maybe draw a picture to finish the story. You might also ask them **how the character or characters feel** in the story.
- You could continue this activity over a number of sessions, revisiting the story, maybe **swapping the cards** to see if the story still makes sense in different places with different characters.
- You may have other ideas for extending this activity.

Box 6.2 Washing line story string activity

to use a voice recorder to record the stories. This will enable you to transcribe them after the session to ensure you have an accurate record. Once the child's **narrative** is written down, the teacher scores the story using the record sheet and selects one or two teaching points to work on in the next session. A scored example of a child's story and possible teaching points can be seen in Figure 6.5. The picture sequences used in the programme were used with permission from Black Sheep Press.

Individual Sessions: Narrative Task Record Sheet

Name_____

Date _____

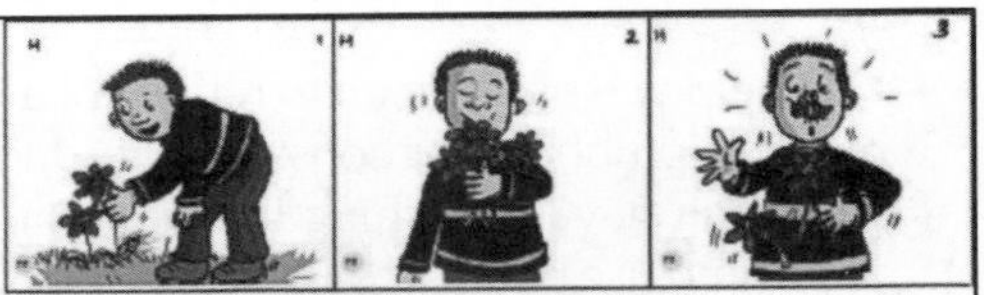

Pictures courtesy of Black Sheep Press

Child's Story	Story Elements
Once there was a little boy. He went for a walk. He saw some flowers. He picked the flowers. He smelled the flowers. A bee stinged him on the nose. The boy dropped the flowers.	Who — (Yes)/No Details.....THE BOY..... Where — Yes/(No) Details............................. When — Yes/(No) Details............................. What — (Yes)/No Details..WALK, flowers, bee Emotion — Yes/(No) Details.............................

Total Number of Words   _35_

Total Number of Connectives   _0_

Connectives Used (tick box if used)

And	
And then	
That	
When	
So	
Because	
Until	
While	
But	
Other (specify)	

Descriptives used (e.g. big, clean, smaller, happy etc):

Little

Figure 6.5 A child's narrative

If we look at the 'story' in Figure 6.5 we can see that the child has managed to include the key information available in the pictures. He has used complete sentences and for the most part he has used the correct grammatical forms except for 'stinged' where he has not used the past tense properly. However, his story lacks **narrative** flow and detail.

The teacher has identified a number of teaching points to work on with the child – this is by no means an exhaustive list but serves as a starting point for the next session. For example, the teacher might talk to the child about how the events in the story are linked and words that can be used to show those links, for example, *why did the boy drop the flowers?* The boy dropped the flowers *because* the bee stung him on the nose. The teacher might ask the child *where* the story took place, for example, *did the boy go for a walk in the woods or in the park?* Could he have gone for a walk on the beach – would he have found flowers there? *When* did the story take place? Could it have taken place in the winter? Would the story have taken place during the day or at night? Would it have been a sunny day or a rainy day?

The teacher might also encourage the child to embellish the story. For example, who was he picking flowers for and why? Perhaps they were for his mum for her birthday, or for his sister because she wasn't feeling well.

In addition to these specific points, the teacher would use the general modelling principle to encourage correct grammatical structure. This story could be revisited in more than one session if there are more teaching points to be raised.

Finally, a story book could be made of the child's stories at the end of the programme to provide the child with a record of their achievements.

SUMMARY

In this chapter we have described the structure of the OL programme and we have provided examples of some of the activities we incorporated in it. The children really enjoyed the sessions, and so did the teaching assistants, but it is worth reflecting for a moment on what worked and why. Given an integrated programme such as the OL programme, it is difficult to evaluate the efficacy of the different component activities; our results show that the children made the most gains in vocabulary knowledge (for the words we taught) and in their use of **grammar**. They also made marginally significant gains in **narrative** skills. Remember gains in these skills were selective (that is, the children who received the P + R programme did not show these benefits). The findings are thought provoking: was it the group sessions that were important for language development or was most of the improvement due to work done in the one-to-one setting? In truth, we just don't know what made our intervention effective, but it did promote oral language skills in those who received it. We will have to leave the question of why and how the OL programme worked to future research.

Chapter 7

Adapting the Programme for Children with Different Needs

Readers of this book may at this point be wondering which intervention would be suitable for a particular child they are teaching or more specifically, whether any particular activities would be suitable for a child they know with special educational needs. In this chapter we emphasize the importance of understanding the learning needs of individual children, and tailoring the content of intervention to meet these needs. This is an example of *personalised learning*, a principle which has been encouraged recently in schools. Building on the positive findings of our **randomised controlled trial** which has already been discussed, two of our smaller research projects have taken this more personalised approach. Here we describe how the basic **Phonology** with Reading (P + R) approach was adapted to meet the needs of two groups of children: children with persistent difficulties in reading accuracy, whose reading had not improved during a first course of intervention and children with Down syndrome.

CHILDREN WHO RESPOND POORLY TO INTERVENTION

Although there is now a good understanding of what makes for successful reading instruction and intervention, it is important to be aware that there are individual differences in how well children will respond to intervention. Children who struggle to benefit from generally effective instructional approaches are sometimes referred to as ***treatment resisters*** or *nonresponders*. Our research team followed up a small group of such children whose reading skills had not improved despite the fact

Developing Language and Literacy: Effective Intervention in the Early Years
By Julia M. Carroll, Claudine Bowyer-Crane, Fiona J. Duff, Charles Hulme, and Margaret J. Snowling
© 2011 John Wiley & Sons, Ltd

that they had received the evidence-based *Reading Intervention* devised by Peter Hatcher and colleagues (discussed in Chapter 2).

Our starting point was to carry out a thorough assessment of each of these children's literacy and literacy-related skills (Duff et al., 2008). From these assessments, it was clear that in addition to their expected difficulties with **phoneme** awareness and letter knowledge, this group of nonresponders also showed weaknesses in *oral language* (e.g. *vocabulary*, and **grammar**). Two case studies are included in Box 7.1 to illustrate this point.

Lizzie

Lizzie is 7 years and 9 months old. She is an outgoing and fun child who loves to please. Sadly, life outside school isn't always stable for Lizzie. Lizzie reads at the level of a child two years younger than her. She can struggle even with simple words, reading *at* as *it* and *out* as *on*, and reduces longer words to manageable sizes (e.g. *running* becomes *rung* and *money* becomes *mig*). We can see though that Lizzie's reading errors are sensible: she is using information about letter-sounds to make her choices. This is also noticeable in her spelling errors, where words like *rollerskate* and *telescope* are reduced to *rollsc* and *telp*.

Lizzie struggles with **phoneme** awareness – a key foundation for reading accurately. She is unable to blend even simple words, and from her errors we can see that she really does struggle to identify sounds in words (the sounds *e-gg* are blended to form *up*; *d-i-s-c* becomes *sockick*). From her attempts at **phoneme** segmentation, we see she has a particular difficulty with middle and end sounds (*tick* is broken down into *t-o* and *cost* to *c-l*). Part of this may be due to a basic problem with remembering speech-sound information: when asked to repeat nonsense words, Lizzie really struggles and performs at the level of a child younger than 4 years old.

In addition, Lizzie shows weaknesses in spoken language skills. Her ability to define words is equivalent to that of a child aged 6 years and 6 months. Lizzie is able to define simple words (e.g. *a shoe is what you put on your foot*), but some words are only partially defined (e.g. *a bell rings when playtime is finished*) or are unknown to her (e.g. *police* and *transform*). Furthermore, her **grammar** skills are very weak, placing her at the level of a child aged 4.5 years. She shows some classic errors, which are like those of much younger children, or children with a language impairment. For example, Lizzie does not always form her verbs properly (e.g. *She fall down the stairs and her glasses broked; The cat just catched the mouse*).

Despite all these difficulties, Lizzie is not generally delayed in development. She is able to process visual information as quickly as her peers, and her attention skills are age-appropriate. Lizzie therefore seems to have particular difficulties with both language and literacy, and might benefit from both aspects being targeted in an intervention.   *(continued)*

Jake

Jake is 7 years and 8 months old. He is lively, cheeky and funny, but you get the sense that he's a little younger than his years. His reading skills are a year and a half behind what is expected for his age. As with Lizzie, Jake is able to use letter-sound knowledge to attempt word reading, and shows evidence of sounding out and blending (e.g. *j-u-m-p... jump, b-ir-d... bird*). However, this approach would not be expected for a child of his age for such simple words, and Jake still shows difficulties with blending (e.g. *b-r-i-ck* becomes *pick* and *h-e-e-l* becomes *hell*). His spelling attempts, while informed by letter-sound knowledge, reveal some difficulties with certain **phonemes** (e.g. *wulsicit* for *rollerskate* and *wantabut* for *roundabout*).

Jake is therefore showing some awareness of sounds in words, though there is room for improvement. For example, his ability to segment **phonemes** is weak (e.g. pet is broken down into b-e and cost into c-o). As with Lizzie, his ability to remember speech-sound information seems impaired; he also performs at a level of children younger than 4 years old.

Jake also shows weaknesses in spoken language. However, this is not always easy to spot as Jake is really a very chatty child. His knowledge of basic words is fine (e.g. *A shoe is where you put them on your feet to keep them warm*). However, if you listen carefully to the content of what Jake says, he sometimes fails to provide key defining features (e.g. *Car – so you can ride in it; Pet – you look after them and stuff*). Also, despite his sometimes lengthy responses, he can struggle to capture the essence of what words mean (e.g. *Transform – In power rangers when they have to fight evil and then they have to transform into power rangers and blast off to fight evil*).

Jake's attention skills are good for his age, but he does show some weaknesses in processing visual information quickly. Jake would also seem to be a child who would benefit from more intervention that targets not just literacy but also language.

Box 7.1 Case studies of children in REVI

Given the broad language and literacy difficulties that these children showed, and using the guiding principle of personalised learning, we created an integrated intervention programme that aimed to promote both written and oral language skills. Our programme has become known as REVI, which stands for *Reading with Vocabulary Intervention*. REVI is broadly a combination of two existing methods of instruction: *Reading Intervention*, which addresses written language weaknesses, and *Robust Vocabulary Instruction* devised by Isabel Beck and colleagues (Beck, McKeown and Kucan, 2002), which targets oral language. REVI was initially devised for teaching assistants (TAs) to work one-to-one with children, but it could easily be adapted for small group work.

Table 7.1   A typical teaching week in REVI

Day	Morning	Afternoon	Approach
1	Session A (15 mins)	Session B (15 mins)	Teaching
2	Session A (15 mins)	Session B (15 mins)	Teaching
3	Session A (15 mins)	Session B (15 mins)	Teaching
4	Session A (15 mins)	Session B (15 mins)	Teaching
5	Session A (15 mins)	Session B (15 mins)	Consolidation

Programme Structure

Originally, REVI ran as a daily intervention over a course of nine weeks. The first four days in every week involved teaching sessions, in which new material was taught; and the fifth day was reserved for *consolidation* sessions, when time was spent revisiting that week's work. Each day of teaching was broken down further into two 15-minute sessions (see Table 7.1). Session A was typically delivered in the morning and Session B during the afternoon. It was reasoned that a 'little and often' approach would encourage more concentrated attention and effective learning. This approach is in keeping with an important principle of learning – distributed practice.

Session A

Session A each morning focused on oral language skills – particularly the development of vocabulary and spoken **narrative**. Reading and writing were also included to allow the children as much practice with literacy as possible. Table 7.2 shows the running order of each teaching session.

Table 7.2   Structure of Session A in REVI

Activity	Brief description
Reading (5 minutes)	Children read a book at the **easy level** (95% accuracy or more), then move on to one at the **instructional level** (90–94% accuracy). TAs take a **running record** of the **instructional level** book.
Vocabulary instruction (5 minutes)	Teaching children the meaning of new words in a rich and **multi-contextual** way.
Narrative writing (5 minutes)	Children use a sequence of pictures as prompts to tell a story. Following some work on the quality of the language, TAs select a small part of the story for the children to write down.

Table 7.3   Structure of Session B in REVI

Activity	Brief description
Recap of new vocabulary (3 minutes)	Recap of the target vocabulary word taught earlier that day in Session A.
Phonological awareness (5 minutes)	Training in understanding that spoken words are made up of separate sounds, by practising phoneme **blending**, phoneme **segmentation** and phoneme **deletion**.
Sight word learning (3 minutes)	Teaching children to read sight words using multi-sensory methods.
Introduce new book (3 minutes)	Introducing children to a new book at the instructional level before they attempt to read it alone, and then again as a **shared reading** activity.
Recap of word knowledge (1 minute)	Children recall the day's target vocabulary word and its meaning, and read the day's target sight word.

Session B

Session B in the afternoons concentrated on improving ***phonological awareness***, with a particular emphasis on ***phoneme***-level work. As will be clear by now, these skills are vital for reading and writing. Children were also guided in how to use phonological skills to help them with literacy tasks. Again, as shown in Table 7.3, the order of the activities was kept constant.

Programme Content

Many of the strategies used in REVI were taken from the Nuffield P + R and Oral Language programmes described in chapters 5 and 6. Detailed information about how to train **phonological awareness** training, reading (including introducing a new book), and **sight word** learning can be found in Chapter 5. We focus here on aspects of the oral language training which were modified for REVI to make the activities suitable for older children.

Narrative Writing Task

The **narrative** writing task was adapted from the **narrative** task featured in the Nuffield Oral Language programme (Chapter 6). Within REVI, its two main purposes were to encourage fluency of oral language and to demonstrate that fluent speaking skills are an important foundation for writing connected text.

The task is made up of three parts. Briefly, children are given a series of linked pictures that are used as a prop from which they can make up a story. While the child narrates the story aloud, the tutor records this in the child's story book. The tutor then asks the child to write out a set amount of the story. Time is then spent on improving the story either in terms of its language quality or **narrative** skills (full details of this task can be found in Chapter 6).

Vocabulary Instruction

The *Robust Vocabulary Instruction* method of Isabel Beck and colleagues (Beck, McKeown and Kucan, 2002) was used to teach children new words to add to their spoken vocabulary. This approach, in which words are encountered in many different contexts, encourages a deep processing of word meanings that goes beyond mere rote learning of definitions. Ultimately, this should lead to richer and more flexible oral language skills (words will be remembered better and used in different ways). Based on the understanding that children's oral language tends to be more advanced than their written language, an important feature of this instructional approach is that it recommends the teaching of sophisticated words (*tier two words*). Tier two words are defined by Isabel Beck and colleagues as 'high-frequency words. . . that offer students more precise or mature ways of referring to ideas they already know about'.

In the context of REVI, the starting point for vocabulary training was the **instructional level** book that was read in the same session. We took a word or a general concept from this book and rephrased it using a tier two word – for example, '*change*' became '*transform*'; '*very old*' became '*ancient*'. Within REVI, a list of books was chosen to suit the reading abilities of the children involved in the project; for each book, two words were generated for targeted vocabulary instruction. The principles used here to train vocabulary can be applied to teaching other words.

Introducing a New Vocabulary Word

Children are introduced to just one new vocabulary word each day. A worked example is shown in Box 7.2. It can be seen that there is an emphasis on multiple encounters with the target word, and in a variety of contexts. This encourages words to be processed in depth, increasing the likelihood that they will be remembered and later used in a flexible way.

Consolidating vocabulary words

An important feature of this approach to teaching vocabulary is that children encounter words many times, and in different contexts. To achieve this, any new target words that are introduced are revisited later on that same day, and also at the end of each week of intervention. Children are asked on a number of occasions to recall the word that they are working on that day. In addition, consolidation sessions are built into the framework of REVI at the end of each week of intervention. In these sessions the children interact with all the words learnt that week through a variety of fun activities. Some ideas are featured in Box 7.3.

This is an example of how to teach a new spoken vocabulary word, based on the framework devised by Isabel Beck and colleagues. Here the word *persist* is introduced, following the reading of *Kipper's Laces* (from the Oxford Reading Tree scheme) in which the main character, Kipper, is learning to tie his own shoelaces.

1. The tutor places the word in the context of the story: 'In the story, Kipper had to keep trying to tie his shoelaces until he had learnt how to do it himself. He had to *persist*'.

2. The child repeats the word to help secure a memory of how it sounds (a phonological representation): 'Say the new word with me, *persist*'.

3. The tutor provides the child with a dictionary definition of the word: 'If you *persist*, you go on doing something even if it is difficult'.

4. The tutor uses the word in alternative contexts: for example, 'Yesterday I was doing some difficult work and I had to *persist* with it until I got it all right.'

5. The child is encouraged to use the word in additional new contexts: 'Tell me about a time that have you had to *persist* with something'.

6. The child repeats the word to reinforce its phonological representation: 'Say our target word, *persist*'.

Box 7.2 Introducing a new spoken vocabulary word

These activities can be used for consolidating all new vocabulary words that have been introduced in a week, and any other words the child is struggling with from previous teaching weeks. The activities must be carefully planned to suit each targeted word. More than one word may be revised through the same activity. These examples are taken, or adapted, from the book *Bringing Words to Life*, by Isabel Beck and colleagues.

Call My Bluff

Give the child three or four possible definitions of a target word, and ask them to choose the right one. For example:

- '*Donate*'
  a) is a type of cake
  b) means to give money or things to help people
  c) is a very rich person
  d) means to be worried or scared about something

(*continued*)

Same or Different?

Ask the child to explain how two target words are similar or different. For example:

- How are these different?
  a) *'Astonished'* vs. *'terrified'*
  b) *'Exhausted'* vs. *'energetic'*

- How are these similar?
  a) *'Greedy'* and *'selfish'*
  b) *'Scrumptious'* and *'delicious'*

Beat the Clock

- Variation A: Design a true/false quiz to test knowledge of the target vocabulary words. Read the statements to the child and ask him to say whether they are true or false. (This could be made more engaging by giving the child true and false cards, or happy and sad faces.) The object is to answer correctly as many questions as possible in just 90 seconds. You could use the same quiz over again and encourage the child to beat his top score, or you could invent new quizzes. For example:
  1. *'Greedy'* people don't each much food: True or false?
  2. *'Groceries'* are things we buy from food shops: True or false?
  3. If you give up easily, you have *'persisted'*: True or false? Etc. . .

The target words can be consolidated in the original context, or any other appropriate context (e.g. 'Greedy' people want lots of money). This true/false format can also be used in a simpler manner to consolidate one or two words, without the time pressure.

- Variation B: For this version of Beat the Clock, the child has to answer a question by choosing the correct target word from a choice of two target words. Invent a list of questions that demand a target word as the answer. Add another target word as a possible "red-herring" answer. Read the questions to the child. (N.B. Make sure the correct word is sometimes placed first, sometimes second.) The object for the child is to answer correctly as many questions as possible in just 90 seconds. Again, the same quiz could be used over again to encourage the child to beat his top score, or new quizzes could be invented. For example:
  1. How would you feel if you were worried about something? *'Anxious'* or *'relieved'*?
  2. How do we describe people who only think of themselves? *'Mischievous'* or *'selfish'*?
  3. Are friends people we *'Admire'* or *'dislike'*?

The target words can be consolidated in the original context, or any other appropriate context. This forced-choice format can also be used in a simpler manner to consolidate one or two words, without the time pressure.

Box 7.3   Consolidating vocabulary words

Consolidating Learning

It is important that children are given the opportunity to recap and reinforce what they have been learning. Weekly consolidation sessions were built into the REVI programme for this purpose. The structure of the consolidation sessions differed from the teaching sessions, though much of the content was similar.

Session A Consolidation

The focus of this was on vocabulary and **narrative** skills. Here, two or three activities were selected that could be used to expand work on **narrative** skills or consolidate target vocabulary words (either new ones from the teaching week, or any with which the child was consistently struggling). The vocabulary activities could be selected from the examples in Box 7.3; some examples of **narrative** activities are featured in Box 7.4.

Story Teller

Simply ask the child to tell a story, and instruct them to include the target vocabulary word(s) that can also be reinforce through this activity. This can be done in a number of ways:

- Ask the child to tell a story about a topic of his choice.
- Use a picture or character from a book as a start point for the child to then tell a story.
- Start the story with a story stem and then ask the child to continue the story. For example, 'It was a dark, cold night and the ground was covered in snow. Everyone was asleep. Then suddenly. . .'
- Set the child a challenge to tell a story that features a target vocabulary word as many times as possible. Reward him or her with a smiley face for every appropriate usage. For example, 'The King was hungry. He was in the mood for a *scrumptious* dinner. The servants brought him some *scrumptious* food. He licked his lips and rubbed his belly. "This is truly *scrumptious!*" he cried. 'The best food I have ever tasted!' The Queen appeared. 'What's so exciting?' she asked. And the King told her all about the wonderful food he had eaten. 'That sounds *scrumptious!*' she said.

You could write down each of the child's stories so that he has his own storybook.

Story Tennis

In this activity, the child and the tutor take it in turns to say a sentence each, or even a word each. Try to incorporate target vocabulary words. This is also a good opportunity for encouraging the use of describing words.

(continued)

For example:

    Tutor: 'Once upon a time there were three boys who decided to go on
                 an adventure.'
    Child: 'They went to explore the spooky woods.'
Or Tutor: 'One''
    Child: ''day'
    Tutor: 'a'
    Child: 'big. . .'

This game may be especially useful for children who have difficulty in telling a lengthy story unaided.

What Happens Next?

Recap the story of a book and ask the child to describe what they think might happen next, if the story could continue. Encourage the child to give reasons and to use target vocabulary words in his or her answers.

Box 7.4   Consolidating narrative skills

Session B consolidation

The emphasis here was on literacy-related skills, with the session breaking down into three sections. Five minutes could be spent on revising target **sight words**, with a chance to expand this knowledge by working on embedding the **sight words** in written sentences. A further 5 minutes could be spent on training **phoneme** awareness. In the final five 5 minutes, the child could re-read their favourite book of the week.

Effectiveness of REVI

Our trial of the REVI programme was a small-scale pilot project of a new method of intervention which trained oral and written language skills in an integrated way. REVI was a nine-week long intervention, consisting of daily one-to-one instruction. Trained TAs delivered the intervention to 12 different 8-year-old children with severe and persisting reading difficulties, whose reading skills had failed to improve despite previous participation in *Reading Intervention* (**treatment non-responders**). In a 6-month period before REVI began, the children showed almost no progress on measures of oral language and literacy during regular classroom instruction. Over the course of REVI, significant improvements were made on measures of reading, **phonological awareness** and broader oral language skills. Pleasingly, these gains were maintained 6 months later. However it should be noted that REVI was by no means a 'cure' for reading difficulties; most children were still classified as poor readers even after receiving this additional intervention and remained in need of ongoing support – as will many such children with severe difficulties.

Feedback from Teaching Assistants

Once REVI had finished, the TAs provided feedback on their experience of the programme.

When asked how successful they thought REVI had been, on average they rated the programme 5 out of a possible 6.

When asked what aspects of REVI they enjoyed, the TAs answered:

- finding a way to support the child;
- working with specific children and seeing improvements;
- seeing children use and think about the reading strategies taught;
- reading and **phonological awareness**; and
- vocabulary words.

All of the TAs felt that their skills had improved as a result of delivering REVI; all of them hoped to gain more training and experience in the future; and all of them were willing to take part in any forthcoming research projects!

READING INTERVENTION FOR CHILDREN WITH DOWN SYNDROME

Learner Profiles of Children with Down Syndrome

Down syndrome is the most common genetic cause of learning difficulties. However, children with Down syndrome often show uneven learner profiles, with varying strengths and weaknesses. Children with Down syndrome tend to have strengths in memory for visual information and in the social use of language, but weaknesses in memory for spoken information and in **expressive language** skills. With respect to reading skills, the ability to read words by sight is often a relative strength, with reading of nonsense words and reading comprehension as relative weaknesses. In the past, children with Down syndrome were typically taught to read using sight-word approaches, such as the 'look and say' method. However, a major limitation of this approach is that it does not equip children with a strategy for tackling new words (sometimes called a self-teaching device). In contrast, this is the main advantage of phonic approaches. Indeed, there is growing evidence that some children with Down syndrome (and other moderate learning difficulties) may benefit from reading instruction that includes **phonics**. Some of this evidence comes from a small-scale study carried out by our research group (Goetz et al., 2008) which has paved the way for a larger randomized control trial that is currently underway.

Tailoring the Reading with Phonology Programme

Fifteen children with Down syndrome, aged between 8 and 14 years old, took part in this study. They all displayed emerging reading skills (could read 5 or more words on a test of early reading) and attended mainstream schools. The intervention programme was delivered by the children's learning support assistants (LSAs). The content of the programme was very similar to that of the Nuffield Phonology with Reading programme. However, some important adaptations were made to suit the learning needs of these children.

More Intense Teaching

Children with Down syndrome tend to show a slower pace of learning than typically developing children. As such, the intervention only included individual teaching sessions (one-to-one with the LSA), compared to the Nuffield programme which alternated between small-group and individual sessions. In addition, each session lasted longer (40 minutes compared with 20 or 30 minutes), in order to dedicate more time to each activity and increase the likelihood that children could engage in the tasks.

More Flexibility

The variations in children's abilities were much wider in this group of children compared with those included in the Nuffield programme. TAs were therefore particularly encouraged to tailor the intervention to their individual child's needs; for example, when certain letter-sounds were already secure, less time would be spent on this section and relatively more time on the higher-level activities (e.g. book reading or **phoneme** awareness).

Speech-Based Work

Mindful of the fact that many children with Down syndrome have difficulties with speech production, speech-based activities were included in the intervention. Louise Nasir, a speech and language therapist, developed a set of exercises to develop oro-motor skills for speech. These exercises were modeled on the Nuffield Dyspraxia Programme (http://www.ndp3.org), and used the Jolly Phonics letter groups as a framework. For example, children would be shown a relevant picture cue from the *Jolly Phonics* material, and practise making the associated speech sound (e.g. 't'). They would then practise making this sound in consonant-vowel (e.g. 'tea') and vowel-consonant (e.g. 'at') combinations. Various games could be played within this structure, for example, lotto and hide and seek with pictures that represent the target sound.

Programme Structure and Content

An overview of the content of the intervention sessions is given in Table 7.4 The intervention alternated between Sessions A and B, which differed slightly in content. Common to both the sessions was book reading, speech-based work, letter or word learning, and a chance to revise previous material. Children received 40 minutes of daily intervention for either 8 or 16 weeks.

Table 7.4 Structure of the Reading with Phonology programme for children with Down syndrome

Session A	Session B
Ice breaker and revision (5 mins)	Revision (5 mins)
Sound of the day: using Jolly Phonics, a letter sound is introduced and paired with a reinforcing action, a story centred around that letter is told and children practise letter formation (10 mins)	Making sounds: practising making speech sounds (10 mins)
Book work: the sound of the day is reinforced during shared reading of a related book; the child is encouraged to listen for the target sounds in words (10 mins)	Sight word vocabulary: learning to recognise a new word by sight (10 mins)
Segmenting and blending: taking apart and putting together the sounds in words that start or end with the sound of the day (10 mins)	Reading books: reading an **easy book** (>94% reading accuracy); re-reading a book at the **instructional level** (90–94% reading accuracy); reading a new book at the **instructional level** (15 mins)
Making sounds: repetition of lists of words (5 mins)	
Plenary: recapping the sound of the day, summary, and reward (2 mins)	

Effectiveness of the Programme for Children with Down Syndrome

The effectiveness of this reading intervention was evaluated by comparing the progress made by two groups of children with Down syndrome: one group received an initial 8 weeks of intervention while the other group simply experienced regular classroom instruction. The group receiving intervention made significantly greater gains in letter knowledge and the ability to read words that are acquired early on by children (but not in a set of words which are mostly acquired later on in development, nor a set of nonsense words). Furthermore, children's progress in reading tended to be faster during the intervention period, compared to an earlier period when they did not receive intervention, and gains that were made tended to be maintained when re-assessed 5 months after the intervention had finished. However, it is important to point out that there was a considerable degree of variation in how successful this intervention was in improving individual children's reading skills, and that gains observed tended to be small.

CONCLUSIONS

In intervention research, we have now reached a good understanding of what works in remediating word reading difficulties; that is, training letter knowledge, **phoneme** awareness, and the linkage between the two in the context of real book reading. However, this approach is not necessarily effective for all children. In this chapter, we have acknowledged that the content or nature of intervention may need to be tailored to fit an individual's needs – personalised learning. For example, we have suggested that children with Down syndrome (characterised by moderate to severe learning difficulties) may benefit from more intense and flexible teaching that might also include speech-based work. Furthermore, it is important to be mindful of the fact that children with reading difficulties may have co-occurring language difficulties, and an integrated intervention that tackles both sets of difficulties may be more appropriate. In fact, as oral language (e.g. vocabulary) is the foundation for **phoneme** awareness, young children with oral language weaknesses are at risk of developing reading difficulties. Such children may therefore benefit from training in oral language prior to the onset of reading instruction. This is an idea we are currently pursuing in our research.

Chapter 8

Programme Delivery: Training, Implementation and Feedback

In this book we have described a number of intervention programmes which we designed for delivery by teaching assistants (TAs). We have shown that each of the programmes is effective in bringing about gains in targeted skills and we have argued that these gains are educationally significant. What we have left unsaid until this point, is that we would not have been able to implement these programmes without the support of schools and more especially the TAs who taught the children. The TAs with whom we worked enabled us to carry out our research and were the vital 'cogs' who enabled us to complete the virtuous circle linking theory with practice. In this chapter we will describe the training the TAs received from the research team and their views of the interventions: what they liked about being involved in the research and what challenges they faced. Finally we ask ourselves, how we can improve the ways in which we, and others, conduct intervention research and how we can keep knowledge of our interventions live in schools?

THE ROLE OF TEACHING ASSISTANTS

As documented in a report prepared by Peter Blatchford and colleagues for the Department for Children, Schools and Families, London (Blatchford et al., 2009), there has been a substantial increase in the number of TAs employed in schools over recent years. Many TAs now support children with Special Educational Needs (SEN) in mainstream schools and a controversial issue is whether it is fair to leave the support of these children, often the most needy and lowest attaining, to lesser qualified teaching staff. However, while there are mixed findings regarding how

Developing Language and Literacy: Effective Intervention in the Early Years
By Julia M. Carroll, Claudine Bowyer-Crane, Fiona J. Duff, Charles Hulme, and Margaret J. Snowling
© 2011 John Wiley & Sons, Ltd

effectively TAs can address the learning needs of children with SENs, there is good evidence that under certain conditions, they can have a positive effect on pupil progress. This is particularly true for the area of literacy. A systematic review by Alison Alborz and colleagues (Alborz et al., 2009) concluded that TAs who are trained and supported in delivering circumscribed interventions can help children with literacy and language difficulties make significant progress in learning. We strongly agree with this conclusion. As you will be aware by now, a variety of evidence from our own research group (see Chapters 2 and 3) demonstrates how effectively TAs can deliver literacy interventions when they are properly trained, prepared and supported. Here, we share information on how we try to achieve this, and on TAs' reflections about the process.

THE TRAINING COURSE

In designing training for our TAs we were mindful of the knowledge which was critical to the successful delivery of the programmes. This knowledge comprises:

- The theoretical background to the programmes
- The rationale for the research (particularly why we had to randomly assign children to different programmes and why it was important not to digress from the content of each arm of the intervention)
- The constructs we use (for example, **phonological awareness**; **narrative skills**)
- The assessment tools (for example, the **running record** and the **narrative** task)
- The in depth coverage of the content and timing of the programmes.

For the Nuffield Phonology + Reading and Oral Language programmes we trained all our teaching assistants during a four-day intensive training course, spending two days on each intervention programme. They also attended a 'refresher' day between the first and the last ten weeks of the programmes (in practice this was held in September after the summer vacation break). Each training day included mini-lectures, workshops and practical assignments, and TAs were introduced to and familiarised with the content of each of the manuals (see Appendixes 8.1 and 8.2). We also made use of a range of handouts.

Induction for Delivery of the Phonology + Reading (P + R) Programme

Box 8.1 shows the outline programme for the course focusing on the P + R programme.

Training started with the 'nuts and bolts' of the programme and hence, we covered the general teaching principles as outlined in Chapter 3 before moving on to describe the structure of the sessions as outlined in Chapter 5. Next we began to flesh out the programme by focusing on specific elements, namely letter

Phonology with Reading Programme Day 1
9.15am	Coffee
9.45am	Welcome and general principles
	Overview of session structure
10.50am	Jolly Phonics
11.35am	**Phonological awareness** theory
12.05pm	Lunch
12.45pm	**Phonological awareness** workshop
1.45pm	Bookwork workshop
2.45pm	Closing remarks and preparation for training day 2

Phonology with Reading Programme Day 2
9.15am	Coffee
9.30am	Assessment theory and practice
	Taking a **running record**
11.45am	Speech development theory
12.15pm	Lunch
1.00pm	Speech development workshop
2.00pm	Reading books
	Sight word workshop
3.00pm	Coffee, questions and plenary

Box 8.1   Training programme for the Phonology and Reading Intervention

knowledge, **phonological awareness** and book reading. We also included sessions on speech development and assessment.

Letter Knowledge

A critical part of the P + R programme was the teaching of letter sounds using the 'Jolly Phonics' programme. We were lucky to have a member of the 'Jolly Phonics' team to come along to our training day to provide an interactive training session in the administration of this part of the programme. TAs were provided with a full introduction to the programme, teaching materials and example teaching methods.

Phonological Awareness

In this section of the training we aimed to cover both theory and practice. First, the TAs were introduced to the concept of a **phoneme** and to the idea that their awareness of the sounds within words might not be as good as they assume! For example, they were asked to decide how many **phonemes** some different words contained, and to pick out the phonemes within unusual words such as witch (which has only 3 **phonemes**) and fox (which has 4 **phonemes**). This was an important first step, because there is a strong tendency (among literate adults) to use letters to lead our decisions about the sounds within words. We then talked about why we focused on segmenting and blending, as shown on the handout in Appendix 8.3. The TAs were also given a page of 'tricky letters and **phonemes**' to help them become aware of common idiosyncrasies within our spelling system. This is included in Appendix 8.4.

Once the TAs felt more comfortable in working with **phonemes**, they were given exercises to practice teaching segmenting and blending, and particularly in using **scaffolding** techniques to help improve segmenting and blending skills. One TA pretended to be a child with a particular level of skill, while another practised tailoring the segmenting and blending tasks to an appropriate level.

Book Reading

We held workshops to tell TAs about book reading activities and to give them the opportunity to try these out. Using handouts (included in Appendixes 8.5 and 8.6) containing guidelines for individual book reading activities, TAs carried out the group exercise shown in Box 8.2.

Group Exercise

Exercise in pairs – pick a book and each take it in turns to go through the stages of reading a new book.
Introduce the book to your partner, go through it and pick out key words.
Ask your partner to read it and try to imagine how you would support a child in this situation
Then re-read the book with your partner.
The reader should try to make a few mistakes to give their partner the oppportunity to practise their use of the reading strategies.
Then swap roles.

Box 8.2   Group activity to help TAs learn about reading a book with a child

Sight Word Reading

Although the core of the programme was systematic **phonics**, we were aware that some children would still need extra help to help them to remember or 'automatise' words to allow rapid retrieval. Thus, in addition to the three core elements of the programme, TAs were given training in teaching **sight words**. Full instructions about how to integrate this work in the programme were also given in the Manual.

During the training days, they used handouts (in Appendix 8.7) during a group exercise, shown in Box 8.3, in which they had to identify strategies to use with particular children.

Group Exercise

Get into small groups of 2 or 3 and look at each case below discussing together how you would deal with the difficulties described.
What materials do you already have that could help you with this activity?
Try to think about the suitability of each approach to the word you are trying to teach i.e. is it easily broken down or does it need a whole word approach? is it easily associated with something the child is familiar with or is it a more abstract word?

Box 8.3   Group activity to support teaching of sight word reading

The cases that we used for them to think about were:

1. John has been presented with the word *'here'* in previous sessions but seems to have difficulties remembering it. What methods might you use to help him?
2. Mary seems to have difficulty remembering the word *'play'*. How might you help her?
3. Andrew cannot remember the word *'look'* – what strategies could you use here?
4. Charlie keeps saying *'it'* when he sees the word *'is'*. What can you do to help him?
5. Anna says *'me'* when she sees the word *'my'* – how can you help?

Speech Development

The initial training also included work on awareness of speech production, to help the TAs support any children who had difficulties in producing particular **phonemes**. We first encouraged TAs to work out how different sounds were produced in the mouth – for example, that 'b' is produced by bringing the lips together, that 's' involves leaving a small gap between the tongue and the roof of the mouth, and that 'th' involves bringing the tongue forward to touch the teeth. An overview of this information was provided in a handout (Appendix 8.8). They could use this information to see whether individual children were forming sounds correctly. We also provided some ideas for helping children improve their sound formation. For example, we provided pictures of items that differed only by a single **phoneme** (such as tea and key) to push children to notice the difference between the two words. Most children were able to produce all of the **phonemes** accurately, and so this was not crucial for them, but it was useful for children with speech production difficulties.

INDUCTION FOR DELIVERY OF THE ORAL LANGUAGE (OL) PROGRAMME

As with the P + R training, the first part of the training for the language programme gave TAs an overview of the programme as a whole, including general principles and session structure in brief. We then moved on to focus on the theoretical background and specific elements of the programme. As the OL programme was more prescribed than the P + R programme, the training focused on providing background and context rather than on specific instructions for tasks – these were contained in the manual. We also tried to give TAs opportunities to gain practical experience with the programme. The timetable for the training is given in Box 8.4.

Oral Language Programme Day 1

Time	Item
9.30am	Introduction
10.00am	General teaching principles
10.30am	An overview of language skills at age 5
10.45am	Coffee
11.00am	Compile manual
12.15pm	Lunch
1.00pm	Assessment
2.00pm	Coffee
2.15pm	Introduction to **narrative** task
3.00pm	Finish

Oral Language Programme Day 2

9.30am	Question and answer session
9.45am	Introduction to individual sessions
10.30am	Coffee
10.45am	Introduction to group sessions
11.30am	Feedback from pilot group sessions
12.00pm	Lunch
12.45pm	Group session workshop
1.45pm	Coffee
2.00pm	Individual session workshop
2.45pm	Tutorial arrangements
3.00pm	Finish

Box 8.4   Timetable for the training days for the Oral Language programme

Theoretical Background

TAs were given a short presentation outlining the language profile of children aged 5 years and highlighting areas of language that the programme was aiming to improve (see Chapter 1 for a discussion of language as a foundation for literacy development).

Vocabulary

We asked TAs to use a method informed by the work of Isobel Beck et al. (2002) for vocabulary instruction. The idea behind this method is to give children frequent opportunities to encounter and use their new vocabulary in a flexible way across different contexts. The way that new words were introduced followed a specific sequence that lent itself well to multi-sensory techniques (see Figure 8.1). After words were introduced, children met them in different contexts during various activities.

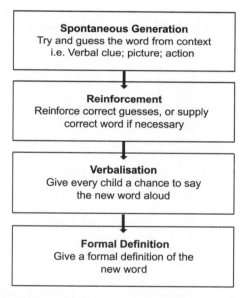

Figure 8.1   Vocabulary method used in the OL programme

Narrative

We wanted TAs to have practical experience of carrying out the **narrative** activity. TAs were asked to complete two exercises. The first exercise focused on transcription. TAs were played a recording of a short story which they had to transcribe. They were than asked to score the transcript using the record sheet provided. We compared scores across groups.

In the second exercise, TAs were given a written transcript for scoring, shown in Appendix 8.9. They also had to discuss in groups the teaching points they had identified. Strategies for addressing these teaching points were fed back to the group.

Planning Sessions in the OL Programme

To help TAs with the task of targeting activities to individual children, we held a planning workshop for individual sessions. In this workshop, TAs were given a record sheet with notes made following a hypothetical group session with 4 children. In small groups TAs had to plan an individual session for at least one of the children. Looking at the notes made in the group session, they needed to identify what skills their child was struggling with. For example, did the child need more practice with active listening? Did they find it difficult to join in with independent speaking? Was there anything about the quality of their speech that needed close attention, for example, use of correct grammatical structures? What activities could be used to address their chosen skills? They also needed to identify whether the child had particular difficulty with any of the vocabulary that had been introduced – did they need more practice using specific words? Were there any words the child had little difficulty with that could be used to boost confidence before moving on to the more difficult words? An example of the activity is given in Figure 8.2.

Record Sheet

Week　　　2　　(3)　　4　　　5　　　6　　　7　　　8　　　9　　　10　　　Session No: 4

Word Types	John	Nadia	Sacha	Max
Nouns				
shoulder	John seems to be ok with this word	Nadia confuses shoulder with elbow	shoulder is fine	not sure whether Max has grasped this word
forehead	John knew this word	forehead is fine	forehead is fine	not confident - says "head"
eyebrow (reinforced)	John still gets eyebrows confused with eyelashes	fine	eyebrows and eyelashes confused	seems ok with eyebrows and eyelashes
eyelashes (reinforced)		fine		
Verbs				
run	John is fine with run - introduce running and ran?	run, running and ran all used correctly. Perhaps think about other contexts i.e water runs.	fine - may want to think about past tense	
Question Form				
who	Understanding ok but has difficulty formulating "who?" questions	able to understand and ask "who?" questions	seems to be ok with both understanding and asking	Not confident in understanding, answering or producing this question form
Skills				
Inferencing	found this quite hard	was ok with this activity	found this quite hard	very quiet - not really sure how he found this

General Comments:

Sacha and John together dominated the group today so it was hard to focus on Max and Nadia.

Max was very quiet today - he doesn't really join in so it is difficult to know whether or not he is happy with the vocabulary etc.

John seems to have problems with some of the vocabulary. He found the inferencing riddles difficult to do. He was very fidgety and distracted today.

He and Sacha were giggling with each other.

Sacha seems to be doing fairly well but did find the inferencing hard. She was not really paying attention today.

Nadia- nouns and verbs fine - might need stretching a bit more so she doesn't get bored. She is coping well with the activities and attending to the

listening rules. She was Best Listener today.

Figure 8.2　An example record sheet from a group session

Refresher Days

The training took place several weeks before the start of the intervention, to allow the TAs to work through the manuals and plan their teaching. Shortly before the start of the intervention, the TAs returned for a 'refresher day' to allow us to answer questions and check on understanding. A second refresher day was held before the start of the term 2 intervention.

At the end of the training, the TAs embarked upon the delivery of the intervention programmes, each TA teaching in both arms of the intervention. Many were nervous, most were apprehensive and a relatively small number felt confident. It was clear that the training course had only been the start of a learning experience for most of the TAs. We planned ongoing support, by way of tutorials which we describe in the next section.

Supporting Teaching Assistants in Tutorials

In order to provide the TAs with ongoing training, to support them and to trouble shoot, we organised fortnightly group tutorials. These also provided feedback to the research team on the content of the programmes and enabled us to monitor the fidelity of delivery.

TAs found the tutorials an ideal opportunity to share challenges and triumphs. Each session started with an opportunity for TAs to talk about their experiences of the previous fortnight.

- Were there any particular issues that they were having difficulty with?
- Was there anything they particularly enjoyed?
- Were they finding it difficult to come up with ideas for helping individual children?
- Had they tried something new that had worked really well?
- Were they finding it difficult to fit the intervention into the school day?

We also used these tutorials to provide extra training for TAs and so, each tutorial had a specific focus:

Tutorial 1. Revision of taking **running records** and **narrative** records
Tutorial 2. Record keeping and behaviour management
Tutorial 3. Syllable counting, segmenting and blending, individual book work, cut up stories
Tutorial 4. Monitoring children's understanding in the Oral Language programme. Feedback from teaching observations
Tutorial 5. General housekeeping session and brief discussion of specific elements of the language programme
Tutorial 6. TA feedback on **narrative** task and record keeping
Tutorial 7. Listening workshop
Tutorial 8. TA demonstrations of activities, and planning related to the observations.
Tutorial 9. Segmenting and blending practice.
Tutorial 10. Observation feedback and TA evaluation.

Many of these tutorial topics were in response to specific issues – for example:

- Many TAs reported that they found the segmenting and blending activities very difficult. In response to this we provided a revision session focusing on **phonological awareness**.
- Many TAs reported that the children they were working with were not working at a level at which they could carry out individual book work. We introduced the cut-up stories activity for these children in which TAs would present one sentence on a strip of paper and give the children cards with the individual words printed on to match to the sentence.

One of the biggest issues for TAs was behaviour management and we provided a session focusing on practical techniques for managing behaviour (see Box 8.5).

Body language, facial expression, eye contact and tone of voice can help to establish control and in turn, a healthy learning environment. It is a matter of sharpening up your presence in the group. Remember, whatever you try needs to feel natural for you!
Top Tips:

- Provide immediate and consistent feedback regarding behaviour.

- Give praise for good behaviour/stickers/sticker chart/certificates and give a reason for giving a reward.

- Try to use a calm, relaxed facial expression that breaks into a smile when appropriate.

- Remain calm, don't debate or argue with child.

- When collecting children from class, make eye contact with each one.

- Establish eye contact when communicating.

- Try to use inclusive language when talking. For example, say 'We learned. . .'

- Use names frequently through each session.

- Simplify complex directions.

- Avoid multiple commands.

- Ensure the child understands before beginning a task.

- Repeat instructions if necessary in a calm, positive manner.

- Help the child to feel comfortable with seeking assistance.

- Initially, the child may need much assistance. Gradually *reduce assistance*.

- Run the session in predictable and organized manner.

(continued)

- Be consistent with daily instructions.
- Develop clear routines for child to follow.
- Control the group without becoming controlling.
- Enforce group rules consistently.
- Develop a signal system with children to gently notify them when they are off task or acting inappropriately.
- Change child seating arrangements if necessary.
- Remember that stress, pressure and fatigue may cause loss of control and behaviour.

Box 8.5   Recommendations for managing behaviour

Additionally, each TA was observed at least once during teaching. This provided an opportunity for the research team to ensure the interventions were being delivered as intended, to evaluate the feasibility of delivering the programme in schools, and to give each TA individual feedback about the observed sessions.

THE VIEWS OF THE TEACHING ASSISTANTS

The main aim of the research that we have reported in this book was to evaluate the efficacy of the two intervention programmes for promoting early language and literacy skills in at-risk children. However, we also hoped that the TAs who delivered the interventions would view their participation in the project as being of benefit to them in terms of their professional development. At the end of the intervention we asked TAs to tell us about their experience of taking part in the project.

We asked TAs to complete a questionnaire about their previous experience, expectations of the project and their evaluation of it. Questions included:

1. How successful do you think the intervention has been?

    Not very successful   Very Successful
                    1   2   3   4   5   6

2. How well do you think the training prepared you for delivering the programme at school?

    Not very well   Very well
                    1   2   3   4   5   6

3. How much have the tutorials helped you in delivering the programme at school?

    Not very much   A great deal
                    1   2   3   4   5   6

4. How competent do you feel delivering the Language Intervention Programme?

> Not Very Competent   Very Competent
>   1   2   3   4   5   6

5. How competent do you feel delivering the Phonological Intervention Programme?

> Not Very Competent   Very Competent
>   1   2   3   4   5   6

We were able to collect questionnaires from 18 of our TAs. The majority were positive in their responses to each of these questions, rating most of the questions at 4 or above. We also asked TAs if they had previous experience of intervention programmes. The majority of the TAs were familiar with intervention programmes, but for four TAs this was a new challenge.

In addition, our colleague Poppy Nash, who had not been involved in the research, held a **focus group** with four TAs. She identified four main themes in her analysis of the transcript, each with 4 to 5 subthemes (see Table 8.1).

Table 8.1   Themes and subthemes emerging from a focus group with TAs

Theme	Subheading
Strengths of intervention project	Support from other school staff
	Support from University of York
	Logistics – delivering the intervention programme
	Personal gains from involvement in the project
	Generalisation of improvements – 'nock on' benefits
Issues arising from the intervention project	Support from other school staff
	Support from the University of York
	Logistics – delivering the intervention programme
	Personal anxieties and challenges
Comparison of the two programmes	Delivery of programmes
	Ending the intervention
	Generalisation of improvements
	General observations
Recommendations based on experience of delivering the intervention	Time management of sessions
	Introduction of new ideas and developments
	Results to schools
	Suggestions for future projects

THEME 1: STRENGTHS OF INTERVENTION PROJECT

Support from Other School Staff

Evidence from teaching assistants indicated that other staff in their school were supportive and positive about the intervention programme. One TA commented about another member of staff: *'I think she realised how much work I'd put into it and appreciated it.'*

Other comments indicated that overall the school was supportive of the delivery of the programmes:

'School was very supportive.'

'I think the class teacher was supportive, I work with two classes and they were both supportive.'

Support from University of York

Comments from TAs indicated that the level of support given by the research team was appropriate and accessible: *'We always felt we could ring in, I often, like it would be a day or two after the tutorial and think, I'm just going to ring and ask them...'*

TAs also felt that the tutorials were a valuable form of support:

'I always came away with something clear in my mind, once we sort of addressed it.'

'As problems emerged, they did sort of address them straight away...'

Tutorials also provided an opportunity for TAs to support each other:

'I think it was reassuring when we used to meet up that we were all doing very much the same.'

'It was an afternoon out, a nice social gathering.'

Day to Day Delivery of the Programmes

Organising the delivery of two intervention programmes in school can be chal-lenging. However, there were elements of delivering the programme that TAs found valuable. In particular, while space was difficult to find in schools, TAs who were able to find a separate space were very positive about it:

'In a separate room away from everybody, which was good because it was quiet.'

'I said [to SENCO] this is what I need, and I was lucky because I got the little room that I could shut the door.'

'It was nice to be able to put my own displays up and keywords on the walls. I had a quiet area in the library and that was great...'

Similarly, the independent nature of the project made it easier for TAs to find the time to carry out the sessions: *'I suppose one thing that was different with this was that certainly for me I was employed by the University and I could say that it was separate hours, whereas with ELS people would say oh don't do it today, we need to do this.'*

Personal Gains from Involvement in the Project

TAs' comments indicated that they gained both personally and professionally from taking part in the project. Many of the comments were centred around gains in knowledge about teaching **phonics**:

> *'A good knowledge of synthetic phonics because it is a big thing at the moment.'*

> *'It's nice to know we're trained in that [synthetic phonics]. Like you say its ownership of the programme isn't it.'*

> *'My Year 1 teacher now leaves me to do phonics all the time.'*

> *'It's a skill that you've learned that you keep with you.'*

Other comments focused on increased recognition of their achievements:

> *'She says oh you know more than me and I don't think I do at all, but it's nice that she thinks that.'*

> *'and she [headteacher] said well you're our expert in that in the school, and if anything else comes up you'll be doing it.'*

TAs also appreciated the opportunity to share their knowledge:

> *'To be able to share skills as well, now I can show the other teachers. It's not just for us, it's sort of extended . . . to the others.'*

> *'and using it in other places in school.'*

One TA commented that she had *'used this for my dissertation'*.

Generalisation of Improvements – 'Knock On' Benefits

In addition to the targeted effects of the programmes, TAs commented on a number of additional benefits to the children:

> *'Confidence – main factor'*

> *'teachers have said that inclusion in the literacy hour has much improved for these children. . . they've got confidence now to join in on the carpet.'*

Similarly, TAs commented that the small group structure of the programme benefited these children:

'When they're in classes there's so many other children, it's having that contact knowing that there's someone there just for you'

'bit of a bond with them really.

TAs commented that the programme was continuing beyond the research project:

'We're starting out again after half-term and training another Teaching Assistant ... so they've decided for our school it's valuable to run again.'

'I think we're going to do a mix of the programme ... we'd like to do a bit of pick and choose.'

In one school, the TA had been using the phonological programme with children who have English as a second language: *'We've got some Polish children so it's working quite well with them.'*

ISSUES ARISING FROM THE INTERVENTION PROJECT

Despite the positive feedback illustrated above, there were some difficulties arising from the programme. Some of these issues are outlined below.

Support from Other School Staff

Not all schools were supportive: *'I think the Head, she was sort of oblivious I think to what was going on, although she must know she initially sent me on it.'*

Some TAs also felt their effort was not recognised: *'I don't think the staff at school understood what we were doing ... resentment that I had, they didn't realise what we're doing at home to deliver it.'*

Support from the University of York

Most of the feedback received with regards to support from the research team was positive. However some TAs did feel inhibited in the group tutorials:

'If you're worried about something and you think there's only you who hasn't picked that up you don't really want to say.'

'There was something as well as at these tutorials that, well, I am quiet and I don't really like to speak out...'

However, a suggestion was offered: *'It would be a good idea for the person to put what they're worried on a piece of paper and give it to staff at the beginning. And they could sort of look through them and then bring those issues up.'*

Logistics – Delivering the Intervention Programme

Many of the difficulties encountered while delivering the programme centred around lack of appropriate space:

> *'I found it difficult because of space.'*

> *'I used to have to walk around the corridors to do individual sessions.'*

> *'and the distraction of people walking past all the time ... because they've got poor concentration anyway. Any little movement ... you've lost them.'*

Time was also an issue, with one TA stating: *'the time aspect because each session was twenty minutes in the afternoon, so I was given an hour block, where I'd get three in, I'd do one at lunchtime... I was often back in late. It was that or cut the sessions short.'*

When sessions took place was an issue for one TA: *'being withdrawn from other things. We tried wherever possible to make it different things they were withdrawn from but...'*

Similarly TAs found preparation time took longer than anticipated and was often done outside of school hours:

> *'I was doing an hour at home on a night.'*

> *'Yes, even towards the end of the 20 weeks, it was still taking that long every night, especially when you've got a child giving you a great, beautifully written story that you then have to transcribe onto paper.'*

Some TAs also allowed sessions to run over: *'I must admit when I was doing the language one, if they were giving me some really good language I would just carry on...'*

There were particular elements of the programme that caused the most anxiety for TAs, specifically the segmenting and blending sections of the P + R programme: *'It was the blending and segmenting that we all had an issue over.'*

Personal Anxieties and Challenges

TAs were very nervous when they first came for training and many were not sure what to expect, with TAs commenting:

> *'I remember that after we had been here on that first day, we did the phonics programme first didn't we, I'm going home thinking Oh No!'*

> *'I think maybe it was after the first day that I knew it was going to be a lot more involved than I thought it was going to be in the first place.'*

Even after training, some TAs were still worried about the programme:

'the assessments were fine because that was very prescriptive. It was when you plan your first session on your own, it was very daunting.'

'It took me at least two or three weeks to settle down to what I was doing.'

Concerns were also expressed about timing within sessions and administration:

'I think time management was a worry... doing it justice...'

'the time factor as well. I think we were all worried we wouldn't be able to deliver in the time that was allocated.'

'sort of worried about the form filling. That's what I worried about.'

SITUATION FOLLOWING INTERVENTION

Following the intervention, TAs made positive comments regarding children's progress:

*'I know one of the Year 1 teachers said to me that she saw such a huge improvement with one of the children's **phonics** skills and where he was with his literacy and everything.'*

'I think they've now got the confidence ... to be shouting out...'

However, negative outcomes were noted in children's behaviour with the cessation of the programme: *'they found that once those children had the one to one in the small group, that they did ... [have] behaviour issues.'*
All of the TAs noted that children found it hard to adjust to losing the small group and individual attention:

'since he's stopped coming he's just gone down again. He's not getting that input every day to keep it in his mind.'

'this particular boy he always wants my attention, because he's had it in the past. I'd say that is probably the main negative.'

COMPARISON OF THE TWO PROGRAMMES

Delivery of Programmes

Feedback from TAs regarding the delivery of the programmes indicated that the P + R programme was the more difficult for TAs to get to grips with: *'It was a lot more technical'*, and *'it was a lot more involved.'*

Similarly the TAs commented that the P + R sessions took longer to deliver:

'I think we maybe found the phonological one a bit more of a rush, especially when they were doing the reading records unless they improved and they made progress, I was finding it really hard to keep to time.'

'They were reading two books and of course they were getting better, you were glad they were getting better, but it was taking more time.'

Ending the Intervention

TAs felt that the OL programme had run its course by the end of the intervention and that the children were ready to finish. The programme had become a bit repetitive and the children were ready to take the skills they had gained and use them in a classroom context:

'I do think the language programme was, for those children who were on it they all made big advances in their language skills . . . but I do think they were ready to finish because it was a bit repetitive to them.'

'children who were on the language, I think they gained a lot in confidence, and maybe that's why they felt they'd had enough.'

*'I think the language is something that is carried on in class more because Year 1 don't teach **phonics**. So **phonics** is going to get dropped a bit, they're not practising that skill.'*

'I like the language, but I think the language could be delivered like the Circle Time sort of thing. I think language would be ideal to use in Circle Time, making up stories, asking people to tell a story by looking at the pictures by having the children in the circle and giving them so many . . . I think that could be carried on in the whole class.'

Conversely, one TA commented that the children in the P + R programme wanted to continue: *'The **phonics**, they wanted to go on. There was plenty to do wasn't there?'*

Delivery of Programmes

TAs commented that the OL programme was easier to deliver but that progress was easier to measure in the P + R programme:

*'the **phonics** was more measurable . . . that child had gone from one to forty-two words in twenty weeks, you know you've done something!'*

'the level of reading as well, you saw them go up in levels of books didn't you, whereas with language you didn't really go up.'

RECOMMENDATIONS BASED ON EXPERIENCE OF DELIVERING THE INTERVENTION

Time Management of Sessions

TAs felt that a little more time would have helped in delivering the sessions to allow for time to organise the children: *'It would have been quite handy just to have that five extra minutes to get to the venue to actually deliver it, because quite often, especially in the summer time, we were outside, and I'd be going outside to find them, hauling them off a bike to go and do their work.'*

Introduction of New Ideas and Developments

TAs took ownership of the programmes and developed many of their own materials: *'We made our own [lower level books] so it was personal to them with photographs . . . initially I was able to carry that into literacy. We made a lot with our key words. We just blu-tacked them on so you could swap them around because mine weren't at the level where they were really reading words, just re-ordering the sentence.'*

Results to Schools

TAs suggested that informing schools of results would help to encourage Heads to continue running the programmes: *'It's this part of the summer term when heads are deciding where they're going to put us and she's talking about running the programme again, so if she can get results . . . it's really worth doing again!'*

Suggestions for Future Projects

TAs felt that more appropriate resources could be supplied: *'Next time – a larger range of books . . . and . . . a lot more lower level books.'*

They also felt that random allocation of children to intervention programmes was not ideal: *'but in future, if it's run again, you'll select the child for that programme'* [not random allocation, but purposefully placing children in the intervention programme that addresses their needs].

Summary of TA Feedback

Overall, TAs found taking part in the programme to be a positive experience from their own point of view and that of the children taking part. Most TAs felt that the children they worked with had progressed in their reading and language skills, and in more general skills like confidence and class participation. A vital factor in the TAs' enjoyment of the programme was the support they received from the research team both during the training and the tutorials, and from each other. Similarly, TAs felt that school support was important both in terms of logistical issues such as space and time, and personal support. One of the striking things to come across from TAs during the programme was the feeling of professional development. Many TAs felt more valued in the schools and were seen as experts in reading and language intervention. Moreover, seeing noticeable improvements in the children they were working with was extremely rewarding. While TAs faced challenges in the delivery of the programmes, their feedback and ideas with regard to these challenges were invaluable for us as researchers and for teaching practitioners.

THE RESPONSES OF THE RESEARCH TEAM TO TA FEEDBACK

We are always heartened by the commitment and enthusiasm of TAs who are involved in our projects. We agree with the review of Alison Alborz et al. (2009) which suggests that TAs can bring about significant improvements in children's language and literacy skills during the course of an intervention programme. From our experience, we also suggest that careful training, support and monitoring of TAs throughout this teaching process is important in order to maximise the benefit and enjoyment for children and TAs alike. Other key issues include ensuring that class teachers and head teachers are aware of the programme and are supportive of the TA in terms of time and space allocations. In the future we will aim to keep the schools informed at every stage of the project, to ensure that this support is maximised. We are also keen to ensure that the skills and commitment of teaching assistants are recognised in their schools and their expertise is kept alive, perhaps through regular events focusing on continuing professional development.

TAKING INTERVENTION RESEARCH FORWARD: REFLECTIONS OF THE RESEARCH TEAM

We believe that a good understanding has been reached concerning how to tackle phonologically-based word reading difficulties in children. However, there is still much to be refined and explored in intervention research. Now that there is general agreement about the core content of phonologically-based reading interventions (that is, training in phonemic awareness and phonic decoding in the context of real book reading) (Torgesen, 2005), attention can turn to more practical matters. For example, rather than completing a set course of intervention (for example, lasting 10 weeks), is it more beneficial to carry on with an intervention until an appropriate level of reading has been reached? This approach might help to reduce the number of children who show poor response to intervention (according to a review by Joe Torgesen of the University of Florida, somewhere between 10 and 46%, [Torgesen, 2000]). It would be important, within such a model, to assess children's performance regularly and critically consider why progress may not be occurring. If a child is failing to respond to an evidence-based intervention that is generally effective with their peers, even after a significant length of time, it may be necessary to change the nature of the educational support. Such principles – of regular assessment, a fair comparison of progress during intervention, and ability to adapt educational input in response to the child – are key features of the Response to Intervention model (Compton et al., 2006).

A related issue concerns how we manage the process of completing an intervention. In most models of interventions, children receive small group or one-to-one support outside the classroom. These attentive and nurturing environments are quite different from the typical classroom scenario. Thus, there are emotional aspects of transition from specialised intervention back to mainstream instruction, of which we should be mindful. In addition, we should be careful to ensure that children are able to generalise their newly developed skills; that is, they should know that they can and should apply the strategies and skills that they learnt in the intervention context to classroom activities. It is important that future research tests out different ways of completing a course of intervention. Possibilities include approaches in which intervention is gradually phased out (slowly reducing the number of days it occurs each week), or those that include supported sessions within the classroom where the child's TA demonstrates how the child's skills can be applied in that context. This second approach was used, though not tested, in the work of Joe Torgesen et al. (2001). We predict that these more scaffolded and tapered models would lead to better maintenance of gains once intervention is removed.

These considerations could also change the way in which TAs are trained and supported. Perhaps it would be useful to include additional training days two-thirds of the way through an intervention, in which TAs are explicitly trained on how to help children to manage the transition away from intervention, and on how to encourage children to generalise their skills. In line with the report by Peter Blatchford, we would like to engage more with teachers as well, and to see more interaction between teachers and TAs during the training for and delivery of interventions. The more that other teaching staff understand about the demands of delivering an intervention programme, the more likely it is that TAs will feel supported and valued – factors that may well be linked to the success of an intervention.

Finally, there is still much to be learnt about interventions that tackle skills beyond word reading. Much less is known about effective ways of training oral language, reading fluency, and reading comprehension; and indeed about comprehensive intervention programmes that might integrate a variety of these skills. The research presented in this book provides insight into some of these issues, but there are many interesting questions that can still be asked and tested in order to take intervention research forward.

References

WORKS CITED

Alborz, A., Pearson, D., Farrell, P., & Howes, A. (2009). *The impact of adult support staff on pupils and mainstream schools: A systematic review of evidence*. London: Department for Children, Schools, and Families.

Beck, I., Perfetti, C., & McKeown, M. (1982). The effects of long-term vocabulary instruction on lexical access and reading comprehension. *Journal of Educational Psychology, 74*, 506–521.

Beck, I. L., McKeown, M. G., & Kucan, L. (2002). *Bringing words to life: robust vocabulary instruction*. New York: The Guildford Press.

Bishop, D. V. M., & Snowling, M. J. (2004). Developmental Dyslexia and Specific Language Impairment: Same or different? *Psychological Bulletin, 130*, 858–888.

Blatchford, P., Bassett, P., Brown, P., Martin, C., Russell, A., & Webster, R. (2009). *Deployment and impact of support staff project*. London: Department for Children, Schools, and Families.

Bowyer-Crane, C., Snowling, M. J., Duff, F., Fieldsend, E., Carroll, J. M., Miles, J. N. V., & Hulme, C. (2008). Improving early language skills: Differential effects of an oral language intervention and a phonology with reading intervention in language delayed young children. *Journal of Child Psychology and Psychiatry, 49*, 422–432.

Bradley, L., & Bryant, P. E. (1983). Categorising sounds and learning to read – a causal connection. *Nature, 301*, 419–421.

Byrne, B. (1998). *The foundation of literacy: The child's acquisition of the alphabetic principle*. Hove: Psychology Press.

Cain, K., & Oakhill, J. (2006). Profiles of children with specific reading comprehension difficulties. *British Journal of Educational Psychology, 76*, 683–696.

Carroll, J. M., Snowling, M. J., Hulme, C., & Stevenson, J. (2003). The development of phonological awareness in pre-school children. *Developmental Psychology, 39*, 913–923.

Clay, M. (1985). *The early detection of reading difficulties* (3rd ed.). Tadworth, Surrey: Heinemann.

Compton, D. L., Fuchs, D., Fuchs, L. S., & Bryant, J. D. (2006). Selecting at-risk readers in first grade for early intervention: A two-year longitudinal study of decision rules and procedures. *Journal of Educational Psychology, 98*, 394–409.

Department for Children, Schools, and Families (DCSF) (2009a). Statistical First Release (SFR) 08/2009. Schools, pupils and their characteristics. January 2009 (Provisional) London: Department for Children, Schools, and Families.

Developing Language and Literacy: Effective Intervention in the Early Years
By Julia M. Carroll, Claudine Bowyer-Crane, Fiona J. Duff, Charles Hulme, and Margaret J. Snowling
© 2011 John Wiley & Sons, Ltd

Department for Children, Schools, and Families (DCSF) (2009b). Statistical First Release (SFR) 31/ 2009. Key Stage 2 Attainment by Pupil Characteristics, in England 2008/09. London: Department for Children, Schools, and Families.

Department for Education and Skills (DES) (2001). *The National Literacy Strategy Early Literacy Support Programme*. London: DfES Publications.

Department for Education and Skills. (2001). *The National Literacy Strategy Framework for Teaching* (DfES Ref 0500/2001). DfES Publications 3.

Duff, F., Fieldsend, E., Bowyer-Crane, C., Hulme, C., Smith, G., Gibbs, S., et al. (2008). Reading with vocabulary intervention: Evaluation of an instruction for children with poor response to reading intervention. *Journal of Research in Reading*, 31, 319–336.

Fuchs, L. S., & Fuchs, D. (2002). Curriculum-based measurement: Describing competence, enhancing outcomes, evaluating treatment effects, and identifying treatment non-responders. *Peabody Journal of Education*, 77, 64–84.

Gleitman, H. (1995). *Psychology* (4th ed). London: W. W. Norton & Company, Inc.

Goetz, K., Hulme, C., Brigstocke, S., Carroll, J., Nasir, L., & Snowling, M. (2008). Training reading and phoneme awareness skills in children with Down Syndrome. *Reading and Writing*, 21(4), 395–412.

Gough, P. B., & Tunmer, W. E. (1986). Decoding, reading and reading disability. *Remedial and Special Education*, 7, 6–10.

Hatcher, P. (2000a). *Sound Linkage* (2nd ed.). London: Whurr.

Hatcher, P. (2000b). Predictors of reading recovery book levels. *Journal of Research in Reading*, 23(11), 67–77.

Hatcher, P. (2006). Phonological awareness and reading intervention. In M. J. Snowling, & J. Stackhouse (eds.), *Dyslexia, speech and language: a practitioner's handbook* (2nd ed., pp. 167–197). London: Whurr.

Hatcher, P., Hulme, C., & Ellis, A. W. (1994). Ameliorating early reading failure by integrating the teaching of reading and phonological skills: the phonological linkage hypothesis. *Child Development*, 65, 41–57.

Hatcher, P. J., Hulme, C., Miles, J. N. V., Carroll, J. M., Hatcher, J., Gibbs, S., et al. (2006). Efficacy of small group reading intervention for beginning readers with reading-delay: a randomized controlled trial. *Journal of Child Psychology & Psychiatry*, 47, 820–827.

Hatcher, P. J., Hulme, C., & Snowling, M. J. (2004). Explicit phonological training combined with reading instruction helps young children at risk of reading failure. *Journal of Child Psychology & Psychiatry*, 45, 338–358.

Herden, K. (2003). Paired associate learning and reading in typically developing children and children with dyslexia. Unpublished doctoral dissertation, University of York.

Hutchinson, J. M., Whiteley, H. E., Smith, C.D., & Connors, L. (2003). The developmental progression of comprehension-related skills in children learning EAL. *Journal of Research in Reading*, 26(1), 19–32.

Iverson, S., & Tunmer, W. E. (1993). Phonological processing skills and the reading recovery programme. *Journal of Educational Psychology*, 85, 112–126.

Moher, D., Schulz, K. F., & Altman, D. G. (2001). The CONSORT statement: revised recommendations for improving the quality of parallel-group randomised trials. *Lancet*, 357, 1191–1194.

Muter, V., Hulme, C., Snowling, M. J., & Stevenson, J. (2004). Phonemes, rimes, vocabulary, and grammatical skills as foundations of early reading development: evidence from a longitudinal study. *Developmental Psychology*, 40, 663–681.

Nation, K. (2005). Children's reading comprehension difficulties. In M. J. Snowling, & C. Hulme (eds.), *The science of reading: A handbook* (pp. 248–266). Oxford: Blackwell.

National Reading Panel (2000). Teaching children to read: an evidence-based assessment of the scientific research literature on reading and its implications for reading instruction. Reports of subgroups. Rockville, MD: NICHD.

Nuffield Dyspraxia Programme. Retrieved 4th August 2010, from http://www.ndp3.org/.

Ripley, K, Barrett, J., & Fleming, P. (2001). *Inclusion for children with speech and language impairments. Accessing the curriculum and promoting personal and social development.* London: David Fulton Publishers.

Rose, J. (2009). *Identifying and teaching children and young people with dyslexia and literacy difficulties* Retrieved 5th July 2009, from http://www.teachernet.gov.uk/wholeschool/sen/

Schroeder, A. (2001) *Time to Talk: A Programme to Develop Oral and Social Interaction Skills for Reception and Key Stage One.* Hyde, Cheshire: LDA.

Snowling, M. J., Gallagher, A., & Frith, U. (2003). Family risk of dyslexia is continuous: individual differences in the precursors of reading skill. *Child Development, 74,* 358–373.

Snowling, M. J., Muter, V., & Carroll, J. M. (2007). Children at family risk of dyslexia: a follow-up in adolescence. *Journal of Child Psychology & Psychiatry, 48,* 609–618.

Torgerson, D., & Torgerson, C. (2008). *Designing randomised trials in health, education and the social sciences: an introduction.* Basingstoke: Palgrave Macmillan.

Torgesen, J.K. (2000). Individual differences in response to early interventions in reading: The lingering problem of treatment resisters. *Learning Disabilities Research & Practice, 15,* 55–64.

Torgesen, J. K. (2005). Recent discoveries on remedial interventions for children with dyslexia. In M. J. Snowling, & C. Hulme (eds.), *The science of reading: A handbook* (pp. 521–537). Oxford: Blackwell Publishing.

Torgesen, J. K., Alexander, A. W., Wagner, R. K., Rashotte, C. A., Voeller, K., & Conway, T. (2001). Intensive remedial instruction for children with severe reading disabilities: immediate and long-term outcomes from two instructional approaches. *Journal of Learning Disabilities, 34,* 33–58, 78.

Vousden, J. I. (2008). Units of English spelling-to-sound mapping: a rational approach to reading instruction. *Applied Cognitive Psychology, 22,* 247–272.

Wechsler, D. (2004). *Wechsler pre-school & primary scale of intelligence - third UK edition (WPPSI-IIIUK)* London: Harcourt Assessment.

FURTHER READING

Language Development and Language Difficulties

Karmiloff, K., & Karmiloff-Smith, A. (2001). *Pathways to language: from fetus to adolescent.* Cambridge, MA: Harvard University Press.

Norbury, C. F., Tomblin, J. B. & Bishop, D. V. M. (eds.). (2008). *Understanding developmental language disorders: From theory to practice* (pp.175–188). Hove, Sussex: Psychology Press.

Snowling, M. J., & Stackhouse, J. (eds.). (2006). *Dyslexia, speech and language: a practitioners handbook* (2nd edn.). London: Wiley.

Reading Development and Dyslexia

Cain, K. (2009). *Reading development and difficulties.* Oxford: Wiley/Blackwell.

Muter, V., & Likierman, H. (2008) *Dyslexia: a parents' guide to dyslexia, dyspraxia and other learning difficulties.* London: Random House.

Thomson, M. (2009) *The psychology of dyslexia: a handbook for teachers, with case studies* (2nd edn.). Oxford: Wiley-Blackwell.

Rose, J. (2009). *Identifying and teaching children and young people with dyslexia and literacy difficulties*. http://www.teachernet.gov.uk/wholeschool/sen/

Snowling, M. J. (2009).Changing concepts of dyslexia: nature, treatment and co-morbidity, *Journal of Child Psychology and Psychiatry, Virtual Issue on-line* (November 2009): http://www.wiley.com/bw/vi.asp?ref=0021-9630&site=1

Useful Websites with Resources

AFASIC: http://www.afasicengland.org.uk/publications/glossary-sheets/
ICAN: http://www.ican.org.uk/Resources.aspx
SpLD Trust: http://www.thedyslexia-spldtrust.org.uk/

Glossary

Articulation: The way in which we make the sounds required for speech.

Case-control studies: A form of evaluation in which a group who have received an intervention are compared with a matched group who have not received the intervention.

Concepts of print: An awareness of how *print* works and how it looks.

Criterion referenced tests: A test is one that that allows test scores to be matched to a statement about the behaviour to be expected of a person with that score. These measures are not standardised but typically provide a list of criteria in a given domain and achievement is monitored against these criteria.

Dyslexia: A reading difficulty characterised by poor decoding skills, usually associated with problems in phoneme awareness, phonological memory and verbal speed of processing. Listening comprehension is typically within the normal range.

Easy book: A book that a child can read independently (at their own level).

Expressive language: The production of words and sentences in a coherent and understandable way to express ideas and communicate with others.

Focus group: A focus group is a form of qualitative research in which a group of people are asked about their perceptions, opinions, beliefs and attitudes towards a given issue.

Formative assessment: In its widest sense, this refers to making someone aware of how they are progressing and can make progress. Teachers use formative assessment to plan teaching against learning objectives.

Grammar: The way words and word parts are combined to convey different meanings.

Developing Language and Literacy: Effective Intervention in the Early Years
By Julia M. Carroll, Claudine Bowyer-Crane, Fiona J. Duff, Charles Hulme, and Margaret J. Snowling
© 2011 John Wiley & Sons, Ltd

Inference: Understanding the meaning of context in a situation or story; generating ideas that are not explicitly written in the story; understanding the social situation, jokes and puns.

Instructional level: The choice of a book that the child can read with 90–94% accuracy.

Invented spelling: A child's attempt to write a word that s/he does not know using letter names or letter sounds.

Morphology: The basic structure of words and the units of meaning (or morphemes) from which they are formed.

Narrative: Sequencing and structuring a story and recounting personal events.

Norm referenced tests: Standardized tests which compare a child's performance to the average for their age.

Onset: Part of the syllable comprising the consonant or consonants that precede the vowel (for example, 'c' in 'cat' or 'cr' in 'cross').

Percentile score: This type of score ranks a child's score in comparison to other children of the same age. A score at the 30th percentile indicates that 30% of the population would score worse than this.

Phoneme: The smallest speech sound in a word. For example, /p/. Phonemes often, but not always, correspond to single letters. For example, the letter 'x' represents two phonemes (/k//s/), while the letters 'th' represent only one.

Phonics: The process of decoding letter sounds and blending them together to make words in reading.

Phonological awareness: The ability to reflect on the sound structure of spoken words.

Phonology: The system that maps speech sounds onto meanings.

Poor comprehenders: Term used to refer to children who decode well but have specific difficulty in understanding what they read.

Pragmatics: The system of language which is concerned with communication and how language is used in context.

Randomised controlled trial: An evaluation of a teaching method or medical treatment in which people are assigned 'at random' to either receive an intervention or to be in a control group.

RCTs: See Randomised Controlled Trial.

Receptive language: Uunderstanding or making sense of what people say.

Rime: The term used to describe the unit of the syllable comprising the vowel and the final consonant or consonants (e.g., the 'at' in 'cat' or the 'ast' in 'mast').

Running record: A form of reading assessment involving verbatim recording of a child reading which is used to identify the set of skills to be taught at the next level.

Scaffolding: A teaching approach whereby you gradually reduce the amount of support you give to the child as they acquire the skill being taught.

Semantics: The system of language concerned with meanings.

Sight word: Printed words that can be read automatically without the need to 'decode'.

Simple view of reading: This theory proposes that reading comprehension is the product of word decoding and linguistic comprehension skills.

Speech difficulty: Refers to a child's difficulty with forming the sounds for speech rather than the content of their language.

Standard scores: A way of expressing a person's performance relative to that of as given population of the same age. The average standard score is set at 100 with a standard deviation of 15. Thus, a score of 85 indicates a moderate level of difficulty (around 16% of children would score at this level or below).

Syntax: Refers to the grammatical structure of sentences.

Treatment non-responder: The term used to describe a child who has not responded to an intervention which is known to be effective. Often these children have significant oral language difficulties.

Appendix 3.1

Reference List for Assessment Tests

Bookbinder, G. E., Vincent, D. & Crumpler, M. (2002). *Salford Sentence Reading Test (Revised)*. London: Hodder Education.

Carey, J., Leitão, S., & Allan, L. (2006). *Squirrel Story Narrative Assessment*. Keighley: Black Sheep Press.

DCSF (2007). *Letters and Sounds: Principles and Practice of High Quality Phonics*. London: DCSF Publications.

Dodd, B., Crosbie, S., McIntosh. B., Teitzel, T., & Ozanne, A. (2000). *Preschool and Primary Inventory of Phonological Awareness*. London: The Psychological Corporation.

Dunn, L. M., Dunn, D. M., Styles, B., & Sewell, J. (2009). *The British Picture Vocabulary Scale III – 3rd Edition*. London: GL Assessment

Hagley, F. (2002). *Suffolk Reading Scale 2*. London: GL Assessment

Leitão, S., & Allan, L. (2003). *Peter and the Cat: Narrative Assessment*. Keighley: Black Sheep Press.

Macmillan Unit. (2000). *The Group Reading Test II*. London: GL Assessment

Muter, V., Hulme, C., & Snowling, M. J. (1997). *Phonological Abilities Test*. London: The Psychological Corporation.

Neale, M.D. (1997). *The Neale Analysis of Reading Ability – Second Revised British Edition*. Windsor: NFER-Nelson.

Renfrew, C. (1991). *The Bus Story* (2nd edn.). Oxford: Speechmark Publishing Ltd.

Renfrew, C. (2003). *The Action Picture Test* (4th edn.). Oxford: Speechmark Publishing Ltd.

Developing Language and Literacy: Effective Intervention in the Early Years
By Julia M. Carroll, Claudine Bowyer-Crane, Fiona J. Duff, Charles Hulme, and Margaret J. Snowling
© 2011 John Wiley & Sons, Ltd

Snowling, M. J., Stothard, S. E., Clarke, P., Bowyer-Crane, C., Harrington, A., Truelove, E., & Hulme, C. (2009). *York Assessment of Reading for Comprehension*. London: GL Assessment.

Wagner, R. K., Torgesen, J. K., & Rashotte, C.A. (1999). *Comprehensive Test of Phonological Processing*. Austin, TX: PRO-ED Publishing, Inc.

Wilkinson G. S., & Robertson, G. J. (2006). *The Wide Range Achievement Test –* 4th Edition. Lutz, FL: Psychological Assessment Resources.

Wechsler, D. (2005). *Wechsler Individual Achievement Test – Second UK Edition (WIAT-II UK)*. London: Pearson Assessment.

Appendix 5.1

List of Books Used for Group Work

Term 1

Sound	Title	Author	Publisher
s	*Sam Sheep Can't Sleep*	P. Cox & S. Cartwright	Usborne
a	*Cat on the Mat*	B. Wildsmith	Oxford University Press
t	*The Tiger Who Came to Tea*	J.Kerr & G. McEwan	Collins Picture Lions
i	*Big Pig on a Dig*	P. Cox & S. Cartwright	Usborne
p	*The Pig in a Pond*	M. Waddell	Walker Books
n	*Not Now Bernard*	D. McKee	Red Fox
k	*Cockatoos*	Q. Blake	Random House
e	*Ted in a Red Bed*	P. Cox & S. Cartwright	Usborne
h	*Hot Hot Hot*	N. Layton	Hodder
r	*Which Witch's Wand Works?*	P. Bernatene	Meadowside
m	*Meg and Mog*	H. Nicoll & J. Pienkowski	Puffin
d	*Little Yellow Digger*	N. Baxter & T. Goffe	Ladybird
g	*Gordon in Charge*	J. Newton	Bloomsbury
o	*Frog on a Log*	P. Cox	Usborne
u	*Fix it Duck*	J. Alborough	Collins Picture Lions
l	*The Very Lazy Ladybird*	I. Finn & J. Tickle	Little Tiger Press
f	*Farmer Duck*	M. Waddell & H. Oxenbury	Walker Books
b	*Don't be a Bully Billy*	P. Cox & J. McCafferty	Usborne

Developing Language and Literacy: Effective Intervention in the Early Years
By Julia M. Carroll, Claudine Bowyer-Crane, Fiona J. Duff, Charles Hulme, and Margaret J. Snowling
© 2011 John Wiley & Sons, Ltd

Term 2

Sound	Title	Author	Publisher
ai	*The Very Lazy Ladybird*	I. Finn & J. Tickle	Little Tiger Press
j	*Jaspers Beanstalk*	M. Inkpen	Hodder
oa	*Toad Makes a Road*	P. Cox	Usborne
ie	*The Tiger Who Came to Tea*	J.Kerr & G. McEwan	Collins Picture Lions
ee	*Sam Sheep Can't Sleep*	P. Cox & S. Cartwright	Usborne
or	*Gordon in Charge*	J. Newton	Bloomsbury
z	*Dear Zoo*	R. Campbell	Picture Puffin
w	*Which Witch's Wand Works?*	P. Bernatene	Meadowside
ng	*Going on a Bearhunt*	M. Rosen & H Oxenbury	Walker Books
v	*The Very Hungry Caterpillar*	E. Carle	Puffin
little oo	*Would you Rather?*	J. Burningham	Red Fox Picture Books
long oo	*Cockatoos*	Q. Blake	Random House
y	*The Big Posh Yacht*	G. Volke	Ravette
x	*Fix it Duck*	J. Alborough	Collins Picture Lions
ch	*I Will Not Ever Never Eat a Tomato*	L. Child	Orchard Books

Appendix 6.1

Example Sessions from the OL Programme

In this book it is only possible to give a flavour of the sessions that we included in the manual from which the teaching assistants worked. Below is an example of an introductory, instruction and consolidation group session. For each session we include an idea of the equipment and materials you will need and we provide some script to use for the various activities. Teachers may wish to substitute activities from other programmes and vary the vocabulary, depending on the needs of the children with whom they are working.

6.1.1   Introduction Session

Overview

- This session will introduce the children to the programme, and the sorts of things that they will be doing in these group sessions.
- The main character and teaching aid, Sam, will be introduced.
- Children will learn how to listen well, and have the opportunity to practise this.
- Children will begin to use some of the vocabulary that will be worked on in greater detail in the coming weeks.

Equipment list

- Digital camera or materials to make name labels and/or self-portraits of each child
- Pictures of Sam's family and house

Developing Language and Literacy: Effective Intervention in the Early Years
By Julia M. Carroll, Claudine Bowyer-Crane, Fiona J. Duff, Charles Hulme, and Margaret J. Snowling
© 2011 John Wiley & Sons, Ltd

- Listening Rules poster
- 'The Three Bears' story and picture cards
- Twinkle, Twinkle, Little Star

Session plan
Introduction:

- Introduce one another and take photographs of each child in the group, or ask them to draw a picture of themselves.
- Then hold up your bag and say 'I have someone very special in this bag. Would you like to meet him?'
- Take Sam out of the bag.
- Introduce Sam and his family.

   'This is Sam. Sam lives at 6 Honeypot Lane.

   He lives with his Mummy and Daddy, and baby brother Ben. They live in a house with a garden and have a pet cat called Mog.

   Sam's best friend is Anna the Rabbit.'

- Ask the following questions about Sam and his family:

   'Can you tell me about our teddy bear?

   What *is the teddy bear's name?*

   Where *does he live?*

   Who *does he live with?*

   Who *is Ben?*

   Is he a boy?

   Who *is Sam's best friend?'*

- Encourage each child to give an answer in a sentence, for example:

   TA: 'What is the teddy bear's name?'

   Child: 'His name is Sam.'

- Introduce the listening rules, using listening rules poster:

   'Sam can show us how to be a good listener.

   Sam says that when you listen you must remember 4 things" (show 4 fingers):

   In the following sentences, insert a child's name into the blank. Make sure each child's name is included.

1. Look with your eyes
   Sam can see . . . . looking. Well done!
   Let us all look at each other with our eyes. Well done!
2. Listen with your ears.
   Sam can see . . . . listening. You are doing very well!
3. Keep still.
   Sam can see . . . . sitting still. You are a good listener!
4. Keep quiet.
   Sam can see . . . . keeping quiet."

Activity 1:

- Ask, 'Who can show Sam that they can be a good listener?'
- Play 'Sam Says . . .' Say, 'We are going to play a game and Sam is looking for the best listener. We are going to play "Sam says". To play this game you have to listen very carefully. I am going to tell you all to make a movement like touch your head, or bend your knees. But, you must only do what I say if I first say "Sam Says". If I don't say "Sam Says", you must stay still. Let's have a practice':

  1 'Sam says touch your head' (make sure all the children are touching their heads. Remind them you have said 'Sam Says'.) Give lots of praise.
  2 'Sam says bend your arm' (again, make sure all the children are bending their arm).
  3 'Touch your nose' (if any of the children touch their nose, remind them you have not said 'Sam Says'.) Give lots of praise.

  Then say, 'Now let's play for real.' Continue as before for a few minutes, for example, 'Sam says point your toes, wiggle your fingers, blink your eyes' etc.

Activity 2:

- Read 'The Three Bears' story. Introduce the words **beginning**, **middle** and **end** of the story, using the appropriate picture cards.
- Say, 'now we are going to listen to a story and afterwards we are going to think what happened at the **beginning**, what happened in the **middle** and what happened at the **end**. Listen carefully.'
- Read the story aloud.
- Then show the children the pictures in sequence.
- Point to picture 1 and say, 'This is the **beginning** of our story.' Describe the picture.
- Point to pictures 2, 3, 4 and 5, and say, 'this is the **middle** of our story.' Describe each picture.
- Point to picture 6 and say, 'this is the **end** of our story.' Describe the picture.

<u>Plenary</u>:

- Ask the children if they can remember what they have done throughout the session, for eample:
  '**What** have we got to remember to be a good **listener**?
  Who can remember what you do when you are **listening**?
  What game did we play? **What** did we do in the game?
  We listened to a story. **What** was the story called?
  Yes, the **title** of the story was 'The Three Bears'
  Who was in the **beginning** of the story?
  What happened in the **middle** of the story?
  Who ran away at the **end** of the story?'
- Nursery Rhyme Time (See Appendix 6.2)
  Say, 'Before we finish today I would like you all to listen to a nursery rhyme. Today our nursery rhyme is Twinkle, Twinkle, Little Star. Who knows this nursery rhyme?' Record responses on your record sheet for each child.
  Say the nursery rhyme out loud. Tell the children they can do the actions if they know them.
- Best Listener: 'Every day, Sam is going to look for the best listener. He will choose the best listener and put their name on the best listener board.' The child then puts his or her photograph or drawing under the correct day on the Best Listener Board.

6.1.2   Instruction Session

Overview

- This session concentrates on teaching two naming words (costume, helmet) and a doing word (tidy)
- Words that describe the position of things will be introduced (outside and inside).
- Last session's words will be reinforced.
- Children will also be encouraged to practise their speaking skills.
- They will revise sequencing and memory by recalling the order of today's activities

Equipment list

- Pictures of people in costumes and helmets
- Pencils and a pencil pot
- 'Where does this belong?' activity cards – to be cut up
- Pictures of a policewoman in uniform and of a buckle
- Coloured A4 paper to make paper aeroplanes
- Paper aeroplane template

Session plan

<u>Introduction</u>:

Introduce the day, for example:

'Today is _____' *(fill in the appropriate day, and point at the day label on the wall/ board)*

'**Who** is going to be the Best Listener **today**?

Who was the Best Listener on _____?' *(fill in the appropriate day, and point to the day label on the wall/board)*

<u>Multi-sensory Learning</u>:

* Naming words: **Costume**; **helmet**:
    1 Ask the children to try and guess the word from context, for example, say the following sentences and ask them to tell you the word that fills the blank, for example:

        Costume: *'I wore a fairy _____ to the fancy dress party'*

        'When we do our Christmas play, we all have to wear a _____'

        Helmet: *'When I cycle I wear my ___ to cover my head'*

        'A fireman has a yellow ___'

        Reinforce correct guesses. Give the children the right answer if they cannot guess it. In this and all similar situations throughout the session, make sure that every child has a go at saying the new words out loud.

    2 Show children real costumes and helmet if possible. Show the children a picture of a costume and a helmet. Ask them to say the words out loud, ensuring each child says both words.
    3 Provide the children with a formal definition, for example:

        '<u>Costume</u>: *clothes you wear when you pretend to be someone else'*

        '<u>Helmet</u>: *a special hat that protects your head'*

* Doing Word: **tidy**
    1 Say, 'What do we do at the end of the day before we go home? Yes, that's right – we **tidy** up.' If children do not respond say, 'What do you do when your bedroom is a mess? That's right, you **tidy** up.'
    2 Tip pencils on the table and say 'Let's **tidy** up the pencils.' Encourage children to say the word **tidy** while picking up the pencils.
* Positional vocabulary: **outside; inside**

    Play 'Where does this belong?' – Show children outside/inside pictures and ask, 'Where does this belong?' Have two piles on the table, or containers – one for outside and one for inside pictures. As the child puts the picture in the correct pile they must say the word '<u>outside</u>' or '<u>inside</u>'.

Reinforcement:

- Naming Words: **Uniform**; **Buckle**: Use the pictures from session one to reinforce the words e.g. '**Who** can remember what this is called?' Make sure each child says both words.
- Doing word: **Fold**: Make paper aeroplanes using template provided. Say, 'We are going to make paper aeroplanes. What do we need to do to the paper to make an aeroplane – we need to **fold** it. I am going to **fold** the paper and I want you to copy me.' Take the children through it step by step. Ask children to say the word '**fold**' as they make their aeroplane.

Speaking:
What would you wear?:

- Say 'We are going to play a game where we have to think about what we would wear. I will tell you that you are going somewhere and you will have to tell me what you would wear. I might say ____, you are going to a party; what would you wear? Or I might say _____, you are going for a walk in the woods, what would you wear?'
- Then say, 'I will go first. At the weekend I am going swimming. I am going to wear my red swimsuit and my blue goggles.'
- Say, 'Now it is your turn.'
- Pick a child and say '___, you are going to a party; what would you wear?'
- Encourage the child to describe their clothing using colour words, etc., for example, if child says 'a dress,' ask what sort of dress?; what colour is it?; how long is it?
- Each child should be given the opportunity to answer a question. Possible questions include:
  You are going to a football match, what would you wear?
  You are going to a wedding, what would you wear?
  You are going to school, what would you wear?
  You are going for a walk, what would you wear?
  You are going to the park, what would you wear?
  You are going to the beach, what would you wear?

Plenary:

- Ask the children if they can remember what they have done throughout the session, encouraging correct sequencing by asking questions such as:
  '**What** did we do **first**?
  What did we do **next**?
  What did we do **last**?'
- As in previous sessions, ask some more specific questions about the work covered today.
- Nursery Rhyme Time: **If time allows**, choose a nursery rhyme to share with the group. You could choose any nursery rhyme, or you could ask a child to choose

their favourite nursery rhyme to share. We have included a list in Appendix 6.2 to give you some examples. Encourage the children to join in with the nursery rhyme.
- Sam chooses today's Best Listener. They then place their picture under the correct day on the Best Listener Board.
- For each child, write one of today's new words on a sticker (perhaps a word that the individual child particularly struggled with), and ask them to put it on their jumper/shirt.

6.1.3   Consolidation Week Session

Overview

- This session aims to reinforce the naming words learnt in the teaching weeks.
- Children will also be introduced to describing words when talking about items of clothing.
- Children will be introduced to story sequencing using simple two sequence picture stories.
- They will revise sequencing and memory by recalling the order of today's activities.

Equipment list

- Naming word pictures from the past two weeks i.e. from 'Pick and Mix People'
- Hanging Out the Washing Game: pictures of washing line and items of clothing
- 'What Happens Next?' Two sequence picture stories

Session plan
Introduction:
Introduce the day, for example 'Today is _____' *(fill in the appropriate day, and point at the day label on the wall/board)*

- '**Who** is going to be the Best Listener **today**?'
- '**Who** was the Best Listener on_____?' *(fill in the appropriate day, and point to the day label on the wall/board)*

Activity 1

- 'I Spy' – play 'I Spy' using the definitions of naming words covered in the teaching sessions.
- Have the pictures displayed on the table or around the classroom and say, for example, 'I spy with my little eye something you wear when you pretend to be someone else' (**costume**).
- The children have to identify the correct picture and say the word aloud.
- Each child should then be encouraged to repeat the correct word.

- Say 'I spy with my little eye . . .'
  1 shoes that cover the leg (**boots**)
  2 the part of a sleeve that goes round your wrist (**cuff**)
  3 the part of a top that covers the arm (**sleeve**)
  4 the part of your coat or trousers you can put things in (**pocket**)
  5 the part of a top that goes round your neck (**collar**)
  6 a special hat that protects your head (**helmet**)
  7 something that helps me do up my belt (**buckle**)
  8 something you wear when you pretend to be someone else (**costume**)
  9 a coat with a hood that keeps you dry in the rain (**anorak**)
  10 clothes that policemen, firemen and nurses wear (**uniform**)

Activity 2:

- 'Hanging Out the Washing' – Say, 'Sam has just done the washing. He has to **hang** it on the line to dry. Here is the washing line. We're going to help Sam **hang** the washing onto the line. Here is all the washing in the washing basket. We have to describe the piece of washing we wish to **hang** on the line. For example, flowery shorts or small striped socks' *(pick up the items as you say them)*.
- Ask each child to take an item out of the basket saying, 'What are you going to **hang** on the line?'
- Ask them to describe it to the rest of the group.

Activity 3:

- 'What happens next?' – Say, 'We are now going to play a game where we need to think about what happens next. I am going to show you a picture and I want you to imagine it is the **beginning** of a story. Then I want you to try and imagine what might happen next in the story.'
- Say, 'I will go first' – pick a pair of cards and show the first card to the children. Explain the situation on the card to the children. Then suggest ideas of what might happen next?
- Select the second card in the pair and say, 'Let's see if I guessed what happened next?' Talk about picture 2.
- Then ask a child to select a pair of cards. Ask them to turn over the first card in the pair and show the rest of the group. Explain the situation to the group. Then ask for ideas about what might happen next.
- When you have been given a few ideas, ask the child to turn over the second card and say, 'Did we guess what happened next?' Talk about picture 2.
- Repeat so each child has a turn at picking a pair of cards.

Plenary:

- Ask the children if they can remember what they have done throughout the session, encouraging correct sequencing by asking questions such as:

'**What** did we do **first**?'
'**What** did we do **next**?'
'**What** did we do **last**?'

- As in previous sessions, ask some more specific questions about the work covered today.
- Nursery Rhyme Time: **If time allows**, choose a nursery rhyme from the list to share with the group. You could ask a child to choose. Encourage the children to join in with the nursery rhyme.
- Sam chooses today's Best Listener. They then place their picture under the correct day on the Best Listener Board.

Appendix 6.2

Nursery Rhyme Time

Twinkle Twinkle Little Star
Twinkle twinkle little star,
How I wonder what you are.
Up above the world so high,
Like a diamond in the sky.
Twinkle twinkle little star,
How I wonder what you are.

Humpty Dumpty
Humpty Dumpty sat on the wall,
Humpty Dumpty had a great fall.
All the king's horses,
And all the king's men,
Couldn't put Humpty together again.

Polly put the kettle on
Polly put the kettle on,
Polly put the kettle on,
Polly put the kettle on,
We'll all have tea.

Sukey take it off again,
Sukey take it off again,
Sukey take it off again,
They've all gone away.

Developing Language and Literacy: Effective Intervention in the Early Years
By Julia M. Carroll, Claudine Bowyer-Crane, Fiona J. Duff, Charles Hulme, and Margaret J. Snowling
© 2011 John Wiley & Sons, Ltd

Little Bo Peep

Little Bo Peep has lost her sheep,
And doesn't know where to find them;
Leave them alone,
And they will come home,
Wagging their tails behind them.

Jack and Jill

Jack and Jill went up the hill,
To fetch a pail of water;
Jack fell down and broke his crown,
And Jill came tumbling after.

Incy Wincy Spider

Incy Wincy Spider climbed up the water spout,
Down came the rain and washed poor Incy out.
Out came the sun and dried up all the rain,
And Incy Wincy Spider climbed up the spout again.

Little Miss Muffet

Little Miss Muffet sat on a tuffet,
Eating her curds and whey;
There came a big spider,
who sat down beside her
And frightened Miss Muffet away!

Two Little Dicky Birds

Two Little dicky birds sitting on a wall,
One named Peter,
One named Paul.
Fly away Peter!
Fly away Paul!
Come back Peter,
Come back Paul.

Hey Diddle Diddle

Hey Diddle Diddle,
The cat and the fiddle,
The cow jumped over the moon;
The little dog laughed to see such fun,
And the dish ran away with the spoon.

Old King Cole

Old King Cole was a merry old soul,
And a merry old soul was he;

He called for his pipe and he called for his bowl,
And he called for his fiddlers three.
Every fiddler, he had a fiddle,
And a very fine fiddle had he;
There's none so rare as can compare,
To King Cole and his fiddlers three!

Tom, Tom, the Piper's son
Tom, Tom, the Piper's son,
Stole a pig and away he run;
The pig was eat,
And Tom was beat,
And Tom went howling down the street.

Appendix 6.3

Resources Used to Develop the Programme

Beck, I. L., McKeown, M. G., & Kucan, L. (2002). *Bringing Words to Life: Robust Vocabulary Instruction.* New York: The Guildford Press.

Rhodes, A. (2001). *Rhodes to Language.* Northumberland, UK: Stass Publications.

Rippon, H. (2002). *Reception Narrative Pack.* Keighley: Black Sheep Press.

Schroeder, A. (2001). *Time to Talk.* Cambridge: LDA.

Developing Language and Literacy: Effective Intervention in the Early Years
By Julia M. Carroll, Claudine Bowyer-Crane, Fiona J. Duff, Charles Hulme, and Margaret J. Snowling
© 2011 John Wiley & Sons, Ltd

Appendix 8.1

The P + R Programme Manual

The main sections of the P + R Manual are listed below:

Developing Language and Literacy: Effective Intervention in the Early Years
By Julia M. Carroll, Claudine Bowyer-Crane, Fiona J. Duff, Charles Hulme, and Margaret J. Snowling
© 2011 John Wiley & Sons, Ltd

Section 4: Consolidation

4.1 Individual Consolidation Sessions
4.2 Group Consolidation Sessions
4.3 Group Consolidation Activities
4.4 Choosing Consolidation Activities to help with Weaknesses

Appendices

Appendix 1: High Frequency Words
Appendix 2: Group Session Reference Sheets
Appendix 3: Basic Concepts in Working with Sounds: Further Activities
Appendix 4: Sight Word Vocabulary Worksheets
Appendix 5: Speech Production Materials: Letter Group 1
Appendix 6: Speech Production Materials: Letter Group 2
Appendix 7: Speech Production Materials: Letter Group 3
Appendix 8: Sound Production Work: Further Information

Appendix 8.2

The OL Programme Manual

The main sections of the OL Manual are listed below:

Section 1: Language intervention programme

1.1 Introduction
1.2 Programme Structure
1.3 General Teaching Principles
1.4 Terms You Will Find Helpful to Know
1.5 Equipment

Section 2: Group sessions

2.1 General Equipment
2.2 Group Session Structure (Teaching Weeks)
2.3 Session by Session Outline

Section 3: Individual sessions

3.1 Structure of Individual Teaching Sessions
3.2 Vocabulary Revision
3.3 **Narrative** Task
3.4 Listening, Speaking and Inferencing

Developing Language and Literacy: Effective Intervention in the Early Years
By Julia M. Carroll, Claudine Bowyer-Crane, Fiona J. Duff, Charles Hulme, and Margaret J. Snowling
© 2011 John Wiley & Sons, Ltd

Section 4: Resources

4.1 Group Session Resources
4.2 Individual Session Resources
4.3 Record Sheets
4.4 Assessment Pack

Appendix 8.3

Handout for Describing Segmenting and Blending

Why Use Segmenting and Blending Activities?

- Learning to read is linked to a child's ability to manipulate sounds in words; that is, a child's 'phonological skills'.
- Children who have problems learning to read often have weak phonological skills.
- Training in phonological skills has been shown to be an effective way of boosting the reading skills of children who are struggling to learn to read, particularly when combined with reading books.
- Blending and Segmenting words into phonemes are two phonological skills that are important for a child's progress in literacy.
- When a child encounters a new word, they need to be able recognise the individual sounds in the word, and then put them together to form a whole word. Thus, blending is important for reading new words.
- When a child is asked to spell a word, they need to be able to break the word up into its constituent phonemes and translate those sounds into letters or letter combinations on the page. Thus, segmenting is important for a child's progress in spelling.

Developing Language and Literacy: Effective Intervention in the Early Years
By Julia M. Carroll, Claudine Bowyer-Crane, Fiona J. Duff, Charles Hulme, and Margaret J. Snowling
© 2011 John Wiley & Sons, Ltd

Appendix 8.4

Examples of Inconsistent Letter-Sound Correspondences

Tricky Letters and Phonemes:

Normally letters and phonemes match up with one another. However, sometimes things are not that simple. Sometimes two letters represent one phoneme, sometimes one letter represents two phonemes and sometimes one letter can represent different phonemes in different places. Here are some common examples.

r – you can't hear it at the end of words (it becomes part of the vowel) e.g. car
h – you can't hear it at the end of words (it becomes part of the vowel) and
    sometimes at the start of words e.g. cheetah, hour
x – marks two phonemes – 'ks' (fox has the same end sounds as socks)
qu – marks two phonemes – 'kw' (queen)
ch and tch (at the end of a word) is just one phoneme (rich, patch, stitch)
th represents two similar sounds, at the beginning of <u>th</u>anks and <u>th</u>eir.
ph – makes a 'ffff' sound (photo)
s – sometimes makes a 'sss' sound, sometimes a 'zzzz' sound (especially in
    the middle or end of words) e.g. miss versus is
c – sometimes makes a 'kkk' sound, sometimes a 'ssss' sound (cactus vs.
    circle)
g – sometimes makes a 'gggg' sound, sometimes a 'jjjj' sound (garage vs.
    ginger)

Developing Language and Literacy: Effective Intervention in the Early Years
By Julia M. Carroll, Claudine Bowyer-Crane, Fiona J. Duff, Charles Hulme, and Margaret J. Snowling
© 2011 John Wiley & Sons, Ltd

y – sometimes makes a 'yyyy' sound, sometimes makes an 'eeeee' sound
   (the sounds at the beginning and end of 'yummy')
kn – makes a 'nnnn' sound (knee)
gn – makes a 'nnnn' sound (gnash)

Silent letters: A lot of words are irregular because of silent letters (knife, island). It is useful to tell children that sometimes there will be silent letters in words.

Appendix 8.5

Handout to Support Individual Book Reading

Individual Book Reading

- At the end of each individual session you will be reading two books with your child.
  - o You will re-read the new book introduced at the end of the last session
  - o You will read a new book chosen by you and the child.
- By doing this activity with books at the **instructional level**, the child will be able to acquire new strategies for reading and hopefully progress to the next levels.
- This activity should take no more than 10 minutes so you are aiming for 5 minutes for each book.

Re-read book introduced at end of previous session.

- This is where you take your **running record** and can decide whether or not children are ready to move on a level.
- Children should move on when they have read a book at the easy level
- This is also an opportunity for you to draw children's attention to text cues to help them avoid errors i.e. the meaning of sentences, the language structure of sentences, letter-sound correspondences
- Add this book to the list (or box) of books the child has read. It helps children to feel they are progressing if they can see how many books they have been reading.

Developing Language and Literacy: Effective Intervention in the Early Years
By Julia M. Carroll, Claudine Bowyer-Crane, Fiona J. Duff, Charles Hulme, and Margaret J. Snowling
© 2011 John Wiley & Sons, Ltd

Introducing new book

- The book should be chosen by you and the child i.e. allow children to select one book from a choice of several, which are all at the appropriate level.
  o Content understood by them
  o Predictable language structure
  o Majority of words within known vocabulary or can be decoded using their existing letter-sound knowledge and decoding strategies.
  o Likely to be read with 90 to 94% accuracy
- The book should be introduced before being read:
  o Introduce book to child and go through it (without reading it) drawing attention to plot and important ideas, pictures, vocabulary children might expect to find i.e. words that could be guessed from context, new words that might come up – do this by suggesting the word and asking the child what sound they might see at the beginning. Then show them the new word.
  o Child should then be encouraged to read the book with minimum help. Encourage child to point to the words as they read, and do this for them if necessary.
  o Stop pointing if child makes an error they should be able to correct.
  o If you encounter a word you think the child might have problems with, offer support i.e. say word loudly, sound the initial letter.
  o Praise children for use of strategies i.e. use of sounding-out, correcting errors etc.
- You should then re-read the book with the child to encourage reading fluency.
  o But still try to give the child a chance to work out difficult words by themselves

Appendix 8.6

Individual Book
Reading Strategies

Individual Book Reading Strategies

1. Encouraging Children's Attention to Text Cues
   - Encourage children to finger point to words in order to establish the one to one relationship between written and spoken words.
   - If this relationship needs reinforcing, ask questions such as
     o Did that match?
     o Were there enough words?

2. Draw child's attention to mistakes made during reading –

   - A low-key approach to getting the children to think about their reading errors might be to say:
     o *'I liked the way you read that. But can you show me the hard bit?'*

   - If the child makes an error you think they should be able to correct you could:
     o Repeat the sentence they have spoken and ask
       'is that right?'
     o Re-read the previous words with fluent phrasing and stop before the error
     o Re-read the previous words, stop before the error and give the first sound of the next word.

Developing Language and Literacy: Effective Intervention in the Early Years
By Julia M. Carroll, Claudine Bowyer-Crane, Fiona J. Duff, Charles Hulme, and Margaret J. Snowling
© 2011 John Wiley & Sons, Ltd

- If children make an error with an unknown word:
  o Prompt them to try and work out what the word might be by asking:
      'Is that right?'
      "How can you work it out?"
  o Tell them the new word and ask
- *'Does it make sense?'*

- *'Would it fit there?'*

- *'Do you think (pointing to the new word) it looks like it?'*

Give children praise for trying to work out error, even if they are not successful

3. Self-Monitoring:
   - Children should be encouraged to monitor their own reading.
   - Ask them to
     o Look at the picture and/or say what has happened in the story
     o Point to each word and predict words they would expect to see
   - Ask questions that encourage children to think about different text cues i.e.
         Meaning – *'Does it make sense?'*
         Syntax – *'Does the sentence sound right?'*
         Auditory – *'What letter sounds would you expect?'*
         Visual – *'Does it look right?'*

   - As children improve, reduce the amount of teaching, modelling and prompting. Ask them to *'Try that again'*, giving them the message that you know they can solve the problem
   - Give children plenty of time to try and self-correct before supporting/ prompting them with an appropriate cue.
   - Always give children plenty of praise for self-correction.

Appendix 8.7

Guidelines for Developing Sight Word Reading

Sight Word Reading

The **sight word** vocabulary section of the session should take no more than 5 minutes. The aim is to gradually build up the number of words the child can recognise by sight.

You should maintain a list of words that the child knows and add to it as you teach each new word.

Your initial assessment should give some idea of the words the child knows.

Remember the following principles: Teach only **one** word at a time and write it in large print.

Use multi-sensory techniques to encourage the child to practice forming the word i.e.

> You write the word on a card or piece of paper and ask the child to trace it, while saying each part
> Ask the child to copy the model of your word
>
> Make the word fluently out of magnetic letters

Developing Language and Literacy: Effective Intervention in the Early Years
By Julia M. Carroll, Claudine Bowyer-Crane, Fiona J. Duff, Charles Hulme, and Margaret J. Snowling
© 2011 John Wiley & Sons, Ltd

Write the word in other media and on other surfaces i.e. with paint, felt-tip pens etc. and on paper, chalkboard, steamed up window, sand tray

Write word many times to bring about fluency and over-learning

After this, include the word in as many reading contexts as possible. You could choose a word that appears in one of the books you are reading for example.

As the child masters each new word, include it on a chart or in a book so that you and the child can keep referring to it.

Once you have taught the child a group of words, you can use activity sheets that encourage the child to read a sentence aloud and fill in a missing word, with your help if appropriate.

Other ideas-

o You could put the words on stickers to put in their workbooks.
o For tricky words, do not attempt to sound them out. Write them down and then box them in to emphasise the fact that you are learning the whole word.

Appendix 8.8

Handout on Speech Production

There are three ways in which consonant sounds can vary:

- Where in the mouth they are made (place)
- How they are made (manner)
- Whether there is voicing (voicing)

1. Where in the mouth.
   Consonants are made by closing a part of the mouth into a small shape. This can happen at the lips, at the teeth, on the roof of the mouth or towards the back.

2. How they are made.
   Sounds are made by either closing the part completely for a moment (a 'stop'), sending air through your nose (a 'nasal'), nearly closing your mouth (a 'fricative') or letting air round the sides of your tongue (a 'glide'). A stop cannot be continued (you have to say 'puh') while the other kinds of sounds can be continued ('sssss').

3. Whether a sound has voicing. Normally, words are voiced, which means that your voice box vibrates while you make the sounds. Sometimes with stops though, you stop the vibration for a moment. These are 'voiceless'.

Developing Language and Literacy: Effective Intervention in the Early Years
By Julia M. Carroll, Claudine Bowyer-Crane, Fiona J. Duff, Charles Hulme, and Margaret J. Snowling
© 2011 John Wiley & Sons, Ltd

Manner			Place			
	Lips	teeth	middle		Back	Far back
Stop	p b		t d		k g	?
Nasal	m		n		ng	
Fricative	f v	th *th*	s z	sh *zz*		h
Glide	W		r l		y	

Other sounds and letters:

Ch = a mixture of t + sh
J = a mixture of d + zz
X = ks
Qu = kw

Appendix 8.9

Example of a Narrative Task

Individual Sessions: Narrative Task Record Sheet

Name_____

Date _____

Child's Story	Story Elements	
Once upon a time there was a girl that was running a tap From a bucket and there was a sponge in and she got the sponge out and walked with the bucket and was washing the car.	Who	Yes/No
	Details..................................	
	Where	Yes/No
	Details..................................	
	When	Yes/No
	Details..................................	
	What	Yes/No
	Details..................................	
	Emotion	Yes/No
	Details..................................	

Total Number of Words   _____

Total Number of Connectives   _____

Connectives Used (tick box if used)

And	
And then	
That	
When	
So	
Because	
Until	
While	
But	
Other (specify)	

Descriptives used (e.g. big, clean, smaller, happy etc):

Developing Language and Literacy: Effective Intervention in the Early Years
By Julia M. Carroll, Claudine Bowyer-Crane, Fiona J. Duff, Charles Hulme, and Margaret J. Snowling
© 2011 John Wiley & Sons, Ltd

Qualitative Analysis: use the scale to indicate your answer (0 = not at all, 6 = very much)	0	1	2	3	4	5	6

	0	1	2	3	4	5	6
Does the story make sense?							
Is there a clear beginning, middle and end?							
Does the child connect the events in the pictures?							
Does the child use story language? (e.g. appropriate openings)							
Does the child use appropriate imagination?							
Does the child use expression?							
Does the child use reported speech? (i.e. the boy he was going for a walk)							
Does the child use direct speech? (i.e. "I am going for a walk" said the boy)							
Does the child use complete sentences?							
Does the child use tense correctly? (or e.g. child says the window **broked**")							
Does the child use the following tenses:							
Present (e.g. I go, you run, he catches)							
Past (e.g. I went, you ran, he has caught)							
Future (e.g. I am going to run, you will go, he will catch)							
Does the child have trouble pronouncing any words?							
If yes, please give examples:							

Index

Developing Language and Literacy: Effective Intervention in the Early Years
By Julia M. Carroll, Claudine Bowyer-Crane, Fiona J. Duff, Charles Hulme, and Margaret J. Snowling
© 2011 John Wiley & Sons, Ltd